People Wasn't Made to Burn

People Wasn't Made to Burn

A True Story of Race, Murder, and Justice in Chicago

Joe Allen

Haymarket Books
Chicago, IL

First published in 2011 by
Haymarket Books
P.O. Box 180165
Chicago, IL 60618
773-583-7884
info@haymarketbooks.org
www.haymarketbooks.org

Trade distribution:
In the US, Consortium Book Sales and Distribution, www.cbsd.com
In the UK, Turnaround Publisher Services, www.turnaround-uk.com
In Canada, Publishers Group Canada, www.pgcbooks.ca
In Australia, Palgrave Macmillan, www.palgravemacmillan.com.au
All other countries, Publishers Group Worldwide, www.pgw.com

ISBN 978-1-60846-126-4

Cover design by Robert Quellos.

Interior photographs of drawings by Ben Shahn, courtesy of the David and Alfred Smart
Museum of Art, University of Chicago; gift of Leon and Marian Despres. Captions drawn
from the words of Annie and James Hickman. Art © Estate of Ben Shahn/Licensed by VAGA,
New York, NY.

This book was published with the generous support of Lannan Foundation and
the Wallace Global Fund.

Printed in the United States by union labor.

Library of Congress Cataloging in Publication data is available.

10 9 8 7 6 5 4 3 2 1

Table of Contents

Above (left to right): Mrs. Annie Hickman, UAW leader Willoughby Abner, James Hickman, and SWP Chicago organizer Mike Bartell. Below (left to right): Mike Myer, William Temple, Sidney Lens, Leon Despres, Willoughby Abner, UAW leader Charles Chiakulas, and Mike Bartell. Annie Hickman is standing in front.

For my mom, dad, and uncle Leo,
and grandpa Joe,
a Boston firefighter

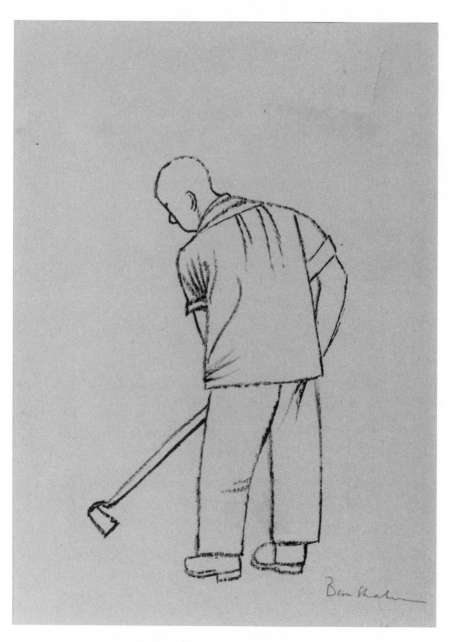

"The landlord furnished everything. But you pays for it. And he don't work."

Introduction
"Nobody knows about it"

"I want you to write about the Hickman case," Frank Fried told me, gripping his cane with one hand and gesturing with the other. "It was the best thing we ever did, and nobody knows about it."

Frank is a retired music impresario. The biggest music event he ever organized was bringing the Beatles to Chicago. Frank has lived in California for many years, and he was in Chicago in spring 2008 to celebrate the birthday of a mutual friend. We were sitting on the porch and talking about his life. He was eighty-one at the time and was facing the possibility of open-heart surgery. I think he was afraid that the Hickman story might completely disappear if the surgery wasn't successful.

"What was the Hickman case?" I asked.

He paused for a moment and said, "Go read the Bartlow Martin article in *Harper's* in 1948, then go from there." I followed his instructions, and this book is the product of two and a half years of research and writing.

The Hickman case is the story of an excruciating family tragedy and a triumph of justice against long odds. The needless deaths of four of the youngest children of James and Annie Hickman in a tenement fire in January 1947, James's shooting and killing of the building's landlord (whom he blamed for the fire), his trial, and the campaign to win his freedom—records of these events have endured mostly as fleeting references or footnotes in books on housing in postwar Chicago. Living memories of them are held almost entirely by a tiny number of the fire's survivors and those who fought for James's freedom. There were only two living as of fall 2010.

Early on I was warned that it might be impossible to write a book about the Hickman case. Writing a book from scratch can be challenging even in the best of circumstances. The Hickman case presented many hurdles: most of the witnesses have passed away, and the Hickman murder trial transcript disappeared long ago. But I settled on an approach that I believe will allow the Hickman story to be told in full for the first time.

I have tried to tell the story first and foremost from the viewpoint of James and Annie Hickman, relying heavily on their testimony at the Cook County coroner's inquest and interviews with the journalist John Bartlow Martin. Their story, of course, was part of a much larger historical drama—the Great Migration, when millions of African Americans traveled north to find a measure of the dignity and freedom that were absent from the Jim Crow South. When they got to Chicago, the Hickmans and others encountered differences in culture and climate—but unfortunately racism still presented obstacles, particularly in access to decent housing.

I have tried to weave the lives of the many people who played a part in the Hickman case into the story, from Mike Bartell of the Socialist Workers Party to UAW leader Willoughby Abner to the movie and stage star Tallulah Bankhead, along with many others. At some points I pause to explain the historical background of the individuals and institutions in the Hickman drama. In an era when newspapers, particularly Black community newspapers, play a diminished role in our lives, the *Chicago Defender*'s work to expose the exploitation and racial oppression of Chicago's Black ghetto and advocate for social change must be explained in depth. The same goes for the radical activists of the Socialist Workers Party who came to Hickman's aid. These are not detours from the main story but integral parts of it.

Much of the history in this book is not easily accessible, and it is certainly given no prominence by those who run the city of Chicago. This year, as every year, millions of tourists will come to Chicago to experience a city that is promoted as both quintessentially "American" and "world class." With their water bottles and digital cameras they will descend on Michigan Avenue and the nearby Millennium Park. They will be shuttled around the city in free buses (for tourists only) between the expensive shopping districts, such as the Magnificent Mile, and the safe confines of the Field Museum, the Shedd Aquarium, the Adler Planetarium, and the Museum of Science and Industry. Few, if any, will venture into the real city. Those who come in search of history will have a hard time finding it. They may unknowingly brush up against it or walk over it, but like everything else in "the City That Works," it will be sanitized and packaged for tourism. The city even frowns on the gangster tour, even though one of the reasons that tourists visit Chicago is the lure of its Prohibition-era gangster past. Al Capone is still the world's best-known Chicago resident.

The best example of this historical packaging is the famed "architecture tour." It is a pleasurable trip along the Chicago River during which enthusiastic volunteers tell an uplifting story of a city that "rose from the flames" of the Great Chicago Fire of 1871, as the great architects of the world helped rebuild it. There is no discussion of such messy issues as the lack of safe, decent housing that led to the fire that destroyed most of the city, or the many fires since then, or, most important, the victims of these fires.

This book is the story of one such fire. Like much of Chicago's real and unsanitized history, the site of the Hickman tragedy is not on the tourist maps and has been literally buried. The building at 1733 West Washburne Avenue no longer exists; it has been buried beneath a nondescript residence for seniors. One warm, lazy summer afternoon I walked to the Near West Side to see the site. Standing there in the bright sunlight, I tried to imagine what the neighborhood must have been like when the Hickmans lived there, but it was almost impossible.

The area has been mauled by institutional expansion for decades. The land just east of what was 1733 West Washburne has become Parking Lot M of the University of Illinois at Chicago (UIC). Across the street is the rear entrance to a UIC research facility, a beige building with blue-tinted windows, typical of ugly corporate and public office buildings built in the 1970s and '80s. To the west and south are several blocks of vacant land peppered along the edges with parking meters. It's a strange sight to behold: it looks as though some powerful weapon that destroys buildings while avoiding any damage to parking meters had been detonated. There is nothing left of the old neighborhood except the elevated train that roars by two stories above the ground. I tried to imagine riding the "L" that cold January night between 11:30 p.m. and midnight. What would I have encountered? An inferno lighting up the night sky? A blare of sirens and glare of lights from fire engines? Neighbors rushing to the building to help? Two figures falling from the top floor? Would I have had a front-row view of a catastrophe or just a hint that something was wrong?

Today as the United States faces the greatest economic and housing crisis since the Great Depression, there is no doubt that circumstances are creating the potential for many James Hickmans. Unscrupulous landlords, real estate companies, and bankers are forcing millions into desperate plights with no options and a growing sense of injustice. Desperate people with little or nothing to lose will take justice into their own hands. Events very much like those of six decades ago could come to mark our own living history.

"I cannot understand how she escaped ... It was a miracle. The Lord was with her."

1

"Mr. Hickman, I hate to tell you this"

At 11:30 p.m. on January 16, 1947, a fire began in the center room of the attic at 1733 West Washburne Avenue, a turn-of-the-century four-story brick building on Chicago's Near West Side. The attic was divided into three separate rooms with a long hallway connecting them. The fire ignited the cheap construction materials used to build the inner walls and quickly spread to the front and back of the attic.

Around the same time, a stranger ran down the darkened stairwell of the apartment building past tenants Albert Jones and Denver Wilson. He told them that there was a fire and urged them to get out, and then he fled into the cold night. Jones and Wilson went to their own apartments and shook their families awake, then banged on the doors of their neighbors, telling everyone to get out. Annie Hickman heard none of this commotion below.

A slow but constant crackling, punctuated by a popping sound, drew Annie out of a deep sleep. She and her six children were sleeping in the front room of the attic. Her husband, James, had left for work just before 9:00 p.m. to work the late shift at Wisconsin Steel. As Annie began to emerge from slumber, she saw what she thought was smoke coming though the cracks around the door to the room. Getting up and moving toward it, she realized that there must be a fire. When she opened the door, a wall of fire and smoke roared inches from her face. Slamming the door shut, she turned and woke all the children. Smoke was filling up the room, and the walls were beginning to disintegrate around them.

Annie's nineteen-year-old son, Charles, sprang to his feet, opened the door, and, jumping through the fire, ran down the stairs.

"Come, Mother, it is not burning down here," he yelled up to her. "Come on!"

"I can't, the fire is in my door," she shouted back, slamming the door shut again to hold back the flames.

But by now the room was completely engulfed in hot smoke that burned Annie's eyes and lungs, making it impossible for her to see. Her four youngest children, Lester (fourteen), Elzina (nine), Sylvester (seven), and Velvina (four), had crawled underneath the bed to escape the smoke. Twenty-year-old Willis, Annie's eldest, leaped to his feet, ran to the door, grabbed the doorknob, and burned his hand. Thinking quickly, he ran to the one window in the room and kicked it out.

"Mother, let's go out the window!"

It was difficult for Annie to see or to breathe, but fire and smoke— hot and thick around her—drove her toward the window, the only way out of the inferno. Jumping out the window would involve a three-story fall onto rock-hard frozen winter ground. Charles had run around to the front of the building, joining the other residents, who had all made it out. He was barely clothed, and the ground under his feet was covered with a thin layer of snow. Neighbors were gathering to offer help. Someone called the fire department.

The growing crowd saw two people—Annie and Willis—climbing out the tiny window of the attic. One neighbor, Rufus Grady, told the rest to get as many blankets as they could to pile below the window and cushion their fall. Hanging on the window ledge and holding his mother's arm, Willis urged her to feel her way to the ledge on the next floor.

"My feet can't reach," she told him. Somehow, though, they both made it to the third floor by clinging to the frame of the building and crawling down it. With Willis's assistance, Annie made it to the second floor. But Willis's grip was slipping. He was afraid that he might fall on his mother. Seeing no other choice, he jumped, breaking his collarbone as he hit the ground. He struggled to his feet and tried to get back into the building to rescue his siblings, but neighbors held him back.

Meanwhile, Annie was still clinging to a ledge on the second floor. With the crowd below urging her to jump onto the pile of blankets, she let go, hitting the pile and injuring her legs. She and Willis were taken to Cook County Hospital in a fire department ambulance.

The four youngest Hickman children never made it out. They huddled together under the bed as the smoke and fire surrounded them and they lost consciousness.

The fire department alarm had rung at 11:43 p.m., alerting firefighters to a fire at 1733 West Washburne. The Chicago Police Department, also alerted, dispatched a patrol wagon and police car with two officers to the scene. Harry Nilson, chief of the Fifteenth Battalion of the Chicago Fire Department, made his way to the fire. When he arrived, he was overwhelmed by what he saw.

"It was a holocaust, it was one mass of fire rolling across the roof," he later testified. By the time he arrived, Annie and Willis had already jumped to safety. The fire burned fast, but it was confined to the attic. Most of the building's roof was destroyed. According to Nilson, it took only five minutes to put out the blaze. The charred, water-soaked attic was now an open space.

"The fire was of no consequence," Nilson reported. "It was the life hazard there we had to cope with."

As he climbed the stairs to the attic, Nilson must have had a terrible foreboding about what he would find. He knew from a previous inspection that children lived in this attic, and four of the Hickman children were missing.

In the attic's front room, firefighters lifted the charred remnants of a mattress to discover the bodies of the four Hickman children. Lester had obviously tried to shield the younger ones from the flames—his body lay over theirs. Even for the most hardened of firefighters it was a difficult sight.

Nilson removed the bodies of the children, and they were carried downstairs and placed in a wagon. The police found clothing for Charles Hickman and took him to the morgue to identify his siblings—Annie and Willis were being treated for their injuries.

James Hickman was working the night shift at Wisconsin Steel on the Far South Side of the city when the fire started. Just before 4:00 a.m., a supervisor told him that the Chicago police had called to say there was "trouble" in his home and he should leave work right away.

"I didn't get no notice at all about no fire on the job," he explained later. The message "just said to me to go to the police station, that I had some trouble in my home."

He was told to report to the police station in the 2200 block of South Dearborn. Taking the No. 5 Cottage Grove bus, James got off where the bus conductor told him he would find the police station. But after wandering around for some time, he could not find it. Confused and frustrated, at around 7:00 a.m. he decided to head home and jumped onto a streetcar on Roosevelt Road. As he approached his building, he saw immediately what the trouble was. James started to enter, but police officers stopped him. Then a neighbor approached and told him the tragic news.

"Mr. Hickman, I hate to tell you this, four of your children is burnt to death."

Six months later, James Hickman would shoot and kill his landlord, David Coleman. By the end of the year, he would be on trial for murder.

"She was born in June and she was beautiful."

2
"We was very anxious to get up north"

James Hickman, son of Charles and Ida Hickman, was born on February 19, 1907, in the countryside near the town of Louisville, located in Winston County in east-central Mississippi. Winston County was a thinly populated region where most people's livelihoods revolved around agriculture and timber. The land had originally belonged to the Choctaw Nation but was ceded to the United States in 1830 under the Treaty of Dancing Rabbit Creek—the first removal treaty carried out under President Andrew Jackson's Indian Removal Act. Though the Civil War had destroyed slavery in Mississippi, the free Black population found themselves without land, subject to the whims of the white planter class—still the largest landowner in the South. Without land of their own, Blacks were forced to work as field hands, tenants, and sharecroppers. The white southern planter, reported one Mississippi newspaper in 1905, was still "lord of all he surveys."

The Hickman family lived a life typical of many Blacks in the postbellum Deep South. They were sharecroppers and raised cotton and corn. Under the sharecropping system, the landowner supplied seed, tools, and animals, while the tenant supplied labor and shared half the crop with the owner. This system forced the tenants to put their whole family to work, young and old alike.

The little that sharecropping families could make from their arduous labors was almost always gone by the end of the year. It was almost impossible for a sharecropping family to save enough to tide them over throughout the season. During the growing season tenants were forced to mortgage their future crops to landlords and merchants in exchange for advances in cash and goods, and landlords routinely shortchanged their tenants. During the so-called slack season every able-bodied member of the family scrambled for additional income—hunting and fishing on the side to put food on the table. But hunger and want were constantly at the door.

The Hickmans' living conditions were spartan at best. James described the family home where he spent his childhood as "a four-room shack." James was the youngest in his family. He had two older brothers, Forest, who died in his teens, and Charles Jr. Like the children of all sharecropping families, the Hickman children went to work at an early age. James was ten years old when he started working in the fields.

When he was twelve, James experienced a religious awakening, and he remained deeply religious for the rest of his life. After his parents separated when he was fourteen, he stayed with his mother. The need for an income forced him to leave school to support her.

At sixteen, he met and married a girl from a nearby sharecropper family, Annie Davis. The two would remain lifelong partners. In 1924, James and Annie's first child, Arlena, was born. Having a child always has a life-changing effect on new parents. In James Hickman's case, his children's health and future were integrally tied to his religious beliefs. After Arlena was born, he made a solemn pledge to God.

"I was the head of this family and to make a support for them, I was a guardian to see them as long as the days I should live on the land." He was seventeen at the time. Eight more children were to follow.

The Hickmans moved from farm to farm in Mississippi, trying to get a slightly better deal from each farmer they sharecropped for. They moved to Fearn Springs, still in Winston County, named for the abundance of ferns (though spelled with an added *a*) in the area by the first non–Native American settlers. The land is hilly and was nicknamed "the Skillet" because of its resemblance to an old-fashioned frying pan. Fearn Springs was a tiny community with a few small churches and a US post office that was part of a general store.

In Fearn Springs the Hickmans started picking cotton. But sharecropping was a game that the sharecropper couldn't win, despite the long days and the enormous physical effort it required. James remembered how the whole setup worked against people like him: "The landlord furnished everything. But you pays for it. And he don't work." One year the Hickmans made only twenty-eight dollars.

Eventually they picked up and moved west to Bolivar County in the Mississippi Delta, where three out of four people were Black. They sharecropped in the delta for seventeen years, but despite the hard work during those long years, Annie lamented, "We could never own the land."

There was a sharp racial divide between those who owned land and those who sharecropped it in Bolivar County. In 1930, whites owned well over 90 percent of the land, and 98 percent of Black farmers were sharecroppers. While slavery had been abolished, the sharecropping system amounted to a new form of servitude where insurmountable debt and the threat of the whip still served in many places to keep Black workers in line. "Under sharecropping and the crop lien," writes historian Neil R. McMillen, "the essential socio-economic patterns of antebellum agriculture survived." The plantation system had simply been reorganized along new lines, and "the great mass of Black agricultural workers remained a dependent, propertyless peasantry, nominally free, but ensnared by poverty, ignorance, and the new servitude of tenantry."

The "best" year the Hickmans had in Bolivar County was in 1942, during the boom years of the Second World War, when they made a grand total of $935.

When Annie and James Hickman's children turned eight or nine, they started working in the fields, rarely attending school for more than four or five months and frequently as little as one month a year. The land-lords frowned on sharecroppers' children going to school. James Hickman recalled one time that the landlord appeared and started "a-grumbling." He barked at Hickman that there was grass growing in the field and he should get his kids out there to weed it. If Hickman didn't, the landlord would hire someone and payment would come out of Hickman's pocket.

"Work is all they look for you to do," Hickman lamented. "They don't look for no school. The plow and such'll keep knowledge out of a person's head."

The Hickmans were fighting an uphill battle. Blacks who attempted to better their condition by purchasing their own land or educating themselves were looked upon suspiciously by whites. "Tenants who as-pired to raise their own cotton on their own land were unwelcome role models for other field hands," writes McMillen, "and their very ambition was evidence that they had ideas beyond their station." Various road-blocks, including loan discrimination and vigilante violence, were used to discourage Blacks from owning land.

The future looked bleak for the Hickman family. Like many Black families, they began to think of escaping the miserable life of sharecrop-ping by migrating north to Chicago.

"We was very anxious to get up north where they [the children] had the opportunity to go to school and all these privileges," Annie re-membered.

After the long bleak years of the Great Depression, prosperity returned to Chicago and the country as a whole with US entry into the Second World War. Chicago's steel mills, meatpacking companies, and manu-facturing industries began to run at full capacity in support of the war effort. The war also gave new impetus to the migration of southern Blacks—which had begun just before the First World War—by the mil-lions to the industrial cities of the North, such as Pittsburgh and Detroit. Chicago, however, held a special attraction for southern migrants. "The mecca was Chicago," declared one Black Mississippian. Chicago was the transportation hub of the country, with rail lines that ran into every national region. It was especially accessible from the South, as the tracks of the Illinois Central Railroad ran through rural Kentucky, Tennessee, Mississippi, and Louisiana. The *Chicago Defender,* the well-known Black newspaper in Chicago, was widely distributed in the Black South by Pullman porters. The *Defender* had been encouraging Black migration to the North for decades.

A young Richard Wright, who would become the premier Black writer of his generation and the author of *Native Son,* arrived in the great metropolis of the Midwest in 1927. He captured the excitement and uncertainty of newly arrived Black sharecroppers in his *12 Million Black Voices*, published in 1941.

"Coming north for a Negro sharecropper involves more strangeness than going to another country." Newly arrived southern Blacks at first had difficulty understanding the speech of the residents of the polyglot city. "The slow southern drawl . . . is superseded by clipped Yankee phrases, phrases spoken with such rapidity and neutrality that we, with our slow ears, have difficulty in understanding." The variety of European immigrants he mingled with dazzled Wright: "Poles, Germans, Swedes, and Italians—we never dreamed that there were so many people in the World!"

Absent were the familiar "For Colored" and "For White" signs that hung over public accommodations throughout the South. But migrants did encounter familiar bigotry and racist violence. In 1919, Chicago had been the scene of one of the worst race riots in the country during the so-called Red Summer. Thirty-eight people died (twenty-three Blacks and fifteen whites), and 537 were injured (two-thirds of these African American), with nearly a thousand residents, mostly Blacks, left homeless by arson.

Housing, however, was the particular sore point for Blacks arriving in Chicago. Many were forced to live in "kitchenettes": dilapidated one-room apartments that in many cases had no heat, electricity, or running water. Wright was furious that so many of his people were forced to live in such hovels. *Voices* includes eight pages of painful photographs and angry prose describing the indescribable conditions in kitchenettes:

When the white folks move, the Bosses of the Buildings let [rent] the property to us at rentals higher than those the whites paid.

Sometimes five or six of us live in a one-room kitchenette, a place where simple folk such as we should never be held captive. A war sets up in our emotions: one part of our feelings tells us that it is good to be in the city, that we have a chance at life here, that we need but turn a corner to become a stranger, that we no longer need bow and dodge at the sight of the Lords of the Land. Another part of our feelings tells us that, in terms of worry and strain, the cost of living in the kitchenettes is too high, that the city heaps too much responsibility upon us and gives too little security in return.

The kitchenette is the author of the glad tidings that the new suckers are in town, ready to be cheated, plundered, and put in their places.

The kitchenette is our prison, our death sentence without a trial, the new form of violence that assaults not only the lone individual, but all of us, in its ceaseless attacks.

The kitchenette, with its filth and foul air, with its one toilet for thirty or more tenants, kills our black babies so fast that in many cities twice as many of them die as white babies.

The kitchenette is the seed bed for scarlet fever, dysentery, typhoid, tuberculosis, gonorrhea, syphillis, pneumonia, and malnutrition.

The kitchenette is the funnel through which our pulverized lives flow to ruin and death on the city pavements, at a profit.

Richard Wright wrote these words before the wartime and postwar conversion of another eighty thousand multiroom apartments into single-room kitchenettes in Chicago.

In April 1944, two months before the Allied invasion of France, James Hickman received his induction notice into the US Navy. But at the last minute he was told not to report for duty because of his age. The military had stopped drafting men older than thirty-six, and James was thirty-seven. He went ahead to Chicago for ten months and worked in a war plant, living with his daughter Arlena. The first member of the family to leave Mississippi, Arlena had married and moved north, where her husband found a job in the Chicago stockyards made internationally infamous by Upton Sinclair's novel *The Jungle*.

Meanwhile the Hickmans' eldest son, Willis, was drafted into the army. James returned to Mississippi, and he and Annie decided that they would leave the state and permanently settle in Chicago. He would go first and bring his family up once he found a job and a place for them to live. James was deeply attached to his youngest children, whose future, he believed, was divinely touched. "These youngest children—I had told them all one night—'It seems like I can see a future for you.' I see in those four children that they possibly would be great men and great women some day . . . I had a vision and the spirit said they would be great."

Back in Chicago, James found a job at Wisconsin Steel on the Far South Side, near the Indiana border. It had originally been known as Brown's Iron and Steel Company, named for its founder, Joseph H. Brown. The mill was built in 1875 on swampland on the west bank of the Calumet River. In 1902, International Harvester bought Brown's Iron and Steel and renamed it Wisconsin Steel. It supplied steel for International Harvester's truck and farm equipment operations. Over the years the mill expanded, eventually taking up nearly 260 acres of land. It was a massive complex.

For the first quarter of the twentieth century, Wisconsin Steel hired only workers of European descent. This contrasted sharply with the steel industry nationally. By 1920, more than 16 percent of the workforce in steel was African American. It wasn't until 1926 that Wisconsin Steel began hiring Mexican workers. But its managers still refused to hire Blacks, even though its parent company, International Harvester, hired them at its other facilities. During the Second World War, the US Fair Employment Practices Commission (FEPC) finally forced Wisconsin Steel to start hiring Black workers. The FEPC had been a direct product of African American labor leader A. Philip Randolph's threatened March on Washington, which had wrenched from a reluctant Franklin Roosevelt a presidential executive order banning discrimination in war plants.

James Hickman started working in the Wisconsin Steel mill in spring 1945 as the war was drawing to a close. Work in a steel mill had a certain kind of glamour then, along with obvious danger. There was a strange and terrible beauty to making steel. It was like working inside a volcano. A 1910 description captures its allure:

> The very size of things—the immensity of the tools, the scale of production—grips the mind with an overwhelming sense of power. Blast furnaces, eighty, ninety, one hundred feet tall, gaunt and insatiable, are continually gaping to admit ton after ton of ore, fuel, and stone. Bessemer converters dazzle the eye with leaping flames. Steel ingots at white heat, weighing thousands of pounds, are carried from place to place and tossed about like toys. Electric cranes pick up steel rails or fifty-foot girders as jauntily as if their tons were ounces.

For a whole generation of Black workers from the rural South, working in a steel mill was like being catapulted from the Middle Ages into the modern world overnight. Hickman was assigned to guiding hot steel as it came off the hotbed. He would have to catch it with a hook as it rolled out and turn it 90 degrees to continue down the line. It was very physically demanding and dangerous work. The danger came from the deadly red-hot heat that burned one's flesh, and from the steel's potential to run off the rolls. Hickman was paid about $1.25 an hour.

In spite of the danger, working at Wisconsin Steel was a big step up from sharecropping. "I could see what I was gittin'. On the farm I'd be charged for a lot of things, I couldn't see what it was for. In the factory work it come to my hand."

Willis served eighteen months in the military before he received a medical discharge. He left for Chicago and began working as a mail handler at the mammoth US Post Office at Van Buren and Canal, west of the Loop.

James, meanwhile, was in a long, frustrating search for housing for his family. At this time the overwhelming bulk of the city's Black population was confined to a narrow sliver of land on the South Side, beginning at Twenty-Second Street (now Cermak) and stretching to Sixty-Second Street between Wentworth and Cottage Grove Avenues. The boundaries of the South Side ghetto were walled off by restrictive "covenants," deals between white homeowners and large institutions stipulating that only whites could buy homes in certain areas. During the First World War the Chicago Real Estate Board had promoted racially restrictive covenants to YMCAs, churches, women's clubs, the many chambers of commerce, and property owners' associations as a way of "protecting" the value of their property from incoming Black families. By the mid-1940s restrictive covenants covered as much as 80 percent of Chicago's residential areas.

The Great Depression followed by wartime rationing meant that by the late 1940s little new residential housing had been built in Chicago. In 1940, 75 percent of Chicago's Black population still lived on the South Side, where the population density in some wards was almost eighty thousand per square mile. It was, however, impossible to hermetically seal up Blacks in the South Side ghetto. In the 1920s they had begun to move into the city's West Side, where they faced the same problems they had on the South Side—overcrowded, dilapidated, rat-infested housing.

In the course of the 1920s, as Jews left the area around Maxwell Street, Blacks moved in to replace them. In many cases it wasn't simply a question of one ethnic or racial group replacing another as the latter climbed the economic ladder. Big real-estate moguls like Sam Homan bought large apartment buildings such as 940–42 West Ohio in Chicago's Little Italy in the early 1940s. He evicted the mostly Italian American residents, cut up the building into smaller apartments with common kitchens and bathrooms, and replaced the previous tenants with Blacks, to whom he charged higher rents. Homan's tactics fanned the flames of racial animosity while reaping a handsome profit. He wasn't alone in doing this. The already overcrowded housing for Chicago's Black community was reaching a crisis situation when it was further exacerbated by the wartime influx of over sixty thousand more Black workers seeking employment in the region's booming mass-production industries. This migration to Chicago continued after the war.

James Hickman worked at night and would leave the mill around 7:00 a.m. It was a long trek from Wisconsin Steel back to the central city. "I would leave the job, and just ride, hunting for a place for my folks," he later recalled. Chicago had an extensive streetcar network that extended into most of its residential and industrial neighborhoods. "Ride and ride, walk and walk. I'd knock on a door and ask. Workin' and lookin'." While new to the city, he wandered into faraway racially segregated neighborhoods. "Sometimes I'd get where they wasn't nothin' but white folks, I'd be the only colored man walkin' down the street. I'd see houses and I didn't know who was living there till I'd knock on the door and they'd say white folks only. They'd tell me which hundred block was for colored. I'd catch the [street]car and go back an' get off there." It is a miracle that racist whites didn't physically assault him and that he wasn't harassed or arrested by Chicago's notoriously racist cops.

Hickman came across plenty of empty apartments for rent. "But they didn't want nobody with children." The housing crunch for Blacks was made worse by the arrival of returning veterans after the war ended. When Blacks tried to move out of the ghetto into predominantly white communities, they faced mob violence. In 1946, for example, a mob of up to three thousand whites rioted to prevent Blacks from moving into temporary housing for veterans on the Southwest Side. Four hundred eighty-five racial housing–related incidents were reported to the Chicago Commission on Human Relations between 1945 and 1950.

The indignities that Hickman suffered began to mount. A public housing project refused him because he had too large a family for its facilities. Real estate offices took his money with promises of finding him housing and found nothing for him. In January 1946 Hickman finally thought he had found a place and brought the whole family up from Mississippi. The wife, the kids, the furniture, and everything else showed up within a day or two of each other. At the last minute, the apartment rental fell through. What were they to do? They crammed themselves into Arlena's apartment, but when her landlord found out how many people were staying there, he told them they had to leave.

In the middle of August, Arlena heard of a possible vacancy at 2720 South Prairie, a building that accepted large families. James and Annie were so anxiously eager that they took a cab there, a luxury that most Blacks couldn't afford. They discovered that no apartment was available at that address, but the man they met at the front door, David Coleman, said that he had an apartment for them on the West Side.

David Coleman, his mother, his wife Sylvestra, and their two children lived at 2720 South Prairie, "a stone relic of Gold Coast splendor." Percy Brown, Coleman's half-brother, also lived in the same building. After the Great Fire of 1871, the rich and powerful had built opulent mansions on Prairie Avenue, including railroad car manufacturer George Pullman and meatpacking pioneer Phillip Armour. It was considered one of the most fashionable neighborhoods in the city, but as the nineteenth century became the twentieth, the rich gradually abandoned their grand homes there for cooler, larger mansions on the north shore of the city. The area became part of the north segment of the South Side Black ghetto. The former stately drawing rooms of the city's elite, and even their butler's pantries, were converted into apartments for Black migrants from the South.

Coleman was a solidly built twenty-five-year-old man in the prime of his life when James Hickman came knocking on his door looking for an apartment. He had been born in a railroad flag stop in the Mississippi Delta on January 22, 1922. Found most often in rural areas, flag stops were rail stations where trains stopped only if there were passengers to be picked up or dropped off. George Coleman, David's father, was a sharecropper, and the family suffered many of the hardships that other sharecropping families faced. David was the youngest of eleven children, all but three of whom died when they were infants. "They just died, I don't know of what," David Coleman's mother sadly recalled. Coleman grew up in a setting similar to Hickman's early home—in fact, only a few miles from him when the Hickmans lived in the delta. Coleman's mother separated from her first husband and met another man named Brown, with whom she had one son, Percy. David started working in the fields when he was twelve years old. He eventually left the fields and became a truck driver. David Coleman married and in 1943 drove his family—his mother, his half-brother, his wife, and their first child—to Chicago, "lured by [the same] tales of freedom and high wartime wages" as the Hickmans.

Chicago was at first a more welcoming city to the Colemans than it was later to the Hickmans. They had arrived when the housing crisis, while terrible, was not as insurmountable as it would be when James Hickman arrived in 1945. David found a job as a mechanic, and Percy started a one-man cab company based in Bronzeville, Chicago's best-known Black neighborhood and home to many Black businesses, advocacy groups, and cultural institutions.

Things seemed to be going in the right direction for the Colemans. "We had a good job and a place to live. No one can do better," David's mother fondly remembered. But his ambitions grew larger the longer he was in Chicago. He wanted to be more than a just a laborer; he wanted to be a businessman. He started dressing like one. Then tragedy struck. David's first wife died while giving birth to their second child. Soon afterward he met and married Sylvestra. The death of his first wife seems to have pushed him even harder to succeed. He trained as a welder and at one point earned $2.10 an hour, a very good wage. But this wasn't enough for his ambitions. He decided that the best route to prosperity would be to own property.

It is not exactly known how David Coleman met Mary Porter Adams, but she would prove to be as fateful for him as he was for James Hickman. Mary Adams was an African American social worker who owned, with her husband, several pieces of property, including a four-story apartment building at 1733 West Washburne. In July 1946, Coleman bought the Washburne property "on contract" from Adams for a total of eight thousand dollars with a three-hundred-dollar down payment. The balance would be paid in monthly installments. Coleman in effect was leasing the property from Adams. He would collect the rents and was responsible for the maintenance of the property, but Adams remained in ultimate control of the building. Why did she lease the building to Coleman? It appears to have been in order to have someone else deal with her increasingly combative tenants. Living conditions in the 1733 West Washburne building were terrible, and the tenants used all legal means available to pressure Adams to fix them.

Julia Rogers was the most vocal and feisty of the building tenants. She later testified that they had been "having lots of trouble with our landlord [Mary Adams] there ever since she has had the place, and she really wants us out, and the whole building has just been having fights and fusses with her." She lived in the second-floor rear apartment with her husband, Elgin Rogers, their two young children, and her brother, who had been recently discharged from the army.

Albert Jones and his family of ten lived in four tiny rooms in the front of the basement—three rooms served as bedrooms and one as a kitchen. All the tenants had problems with David Coleman and Mary Adams. Julia Rogers and other tenants had a heated confrontation with Adams after running into her at the Office of Price Administration (OPA), the mammoth federal agency created during the Second World War to regulate prices, including rents.

On any given day, the OPA's office in the Loop was packed with hundreds of renters, housewives, landlords, and an assorted variety of businessmen battling over price and rent increases. Rogers and a group of tenants saw Adams in the hallway outside a hearing room, where they demanded to know what she was going to do about the unsafe conditions in her building. Rogers pointedly asked Adams whether she cared at all about the safety of the children living there. "She said that the place was not her concern and our children was not her concern. It was just our troubles."

The situation got worse for the tenants after Coleman took over. In July 1946, Coleman made his first appearance at the building. He showed up midmorning with a small group of carpenters and construction material. Almost all the male tenants were at work. Julia Rogers went outside to see who was in charge. She asked Coleman who he was, and he declared himself to be the landlord. Rogers smelled a rat. Coleman said he was there to do some repair work. Right away she suspected that he and his men were there to cut the apartments into kitchenettes.

Rogers called out all the women in the building, and they stopped Coleman and his men from entering. Coleman tried several more times but was foiled each time by Rogers and the others. "We didn't let him in. Every time he came in, we would get out in the hall. He would always know we were just women at home, and we'd go out there and stick together." Coleman became enraged.

Rogers ran into him another morning as she was going down the steps to the second floor. He had been hoping to catch her alone. He stopped her on the stairwell and announced, "Well, I will get you out if it takes fire."

James and Annie Hickman were unaware of any of this when they took a streetcar with David Coleman to 1733 West Washburne. Coleman first showed them a basement apartment for fifty dollars a month. "The water was half a leg deep in the basement . . . no windows, no lights, no nothing in there." Hickman declined the basement apartment. Coleman quickly offered him an attic apartment for six dollars a week until a space on the second floor became free at the beginning of September.

"We walked up the stairs. It was so dark," Hickman later testified, "we almost had to feel our way."

It was a small attic room that adults could barely stand up in, and there was no electricity, no gas, and only one window. But the Hickmans needed shelter for their children. So despite their reservations, they told Coleman that they would take the attic space with the expectation that the second-floor apartment would be theirs soon. They gave Coleman one hundred dollars in advance and moved in on August 21, 1946.

The Hickmans moved in during a mild break in the usual sweltering summer weather that envelops Chicago. The apartment was 25 by 15 feet, with two beds separated by a narrow aisle. Annie and James shared one bed, and the four youngest children, Lester, Elzina, Sylvester, and Velvina, shared the other. With only one small window for ventilation and with the sun beating down on the roof all day, it was a suffocating place.

"No owner, lessee, or keeper of any tenement, house, lodging house, or boarding house shall cause or allow the same to be to be overcrowded, or cause or allow so great a number of persons to dwell, be or sleep in any such house, or any portion thereof to cause any danger or detriment to health," read the Municipal Code of Chicago at the time. Six persons in one room was clearly a serious code violation. Given the lack of electricity and running water, the Hickmans had to go down to the floor below them to get water from a neighbor to cook and clean with; they cooked on a Kenmore two-burner stove a few footsteps from their beds. At a local store James bought two lamps to light the room, both fueled by kerosene. A two-foot-wide stairwell connected the third floor to the attic, which had been cut up into three one-room apartments. There was no fire escape.

"I don't like this place," James told Annie when they first saw it. "I don't either," she told him, "but surely we can stay here, because we ain't got no place."

Nine days came and went, and there was no word from Coleman about their moving into the promised second-floor apartment, so Hickman decided to go looking for him. He found Coleman at his home and was told that this apartment wouldn't be available until September 18, more than two weeks away. Hickman knew that something wasn't right, but he had no choice but to wait. September 18 came and went, and the apartment still wasn't available. He again went to confront Coleman and demanded his hundred-dollar deposit back so he could look for another place. If he didn't get it, he said, he would have Coleman arrested. "I won't pay you," Coleman barked. Hickman then threatened to take Coleman to court. At this point Coleman threatened to burn Hickman and his family out. "He said he had a man on the East Side ready to burn the place up if I had him arrested," Hickman later reported. "He said go ahead and have me arrested, I would be sorry."

Annie and James talked the situation over and decided that they had no choice but to go to the police. This was a difficult decision for a Black couple new to the city. In Mississippi, where they had lived most of their lives, the police and county sheriffs were to be avoided at all costs. They were the ones, in most cases, who led the lynch mobs, robbed Blacks at gunpoint, and enforced the plantation bosses' rules. The Chicago police were no less brutal, corrupt, and disrespectful to Black people, but Annie and James didn't want to be swindled out of their deposit. And now Coleman was threatening to burn them out. They were clearly dealing with a dangerous man.

Together they went to the local police station and took out a warrant for David Coleman's arrest. Nothing happened. The police never acted on the warrant. Coleman was not arrested, the Hickmans never got their money back, and they remained stuck in the one-room attic apartment. James Hickman believed that Mary Adams had hired Coleman to intimidate her tenants, "to beat the people out of their money."

David Coleman seemed to be under enormous pressure to accumulate a large amount of money fast. In October, he "leased" the basement front apartment to Albert Jones for a year. Jones paid him three hundred dollars in advance, the equivalent of six months' rent. Coleman told him he could move in on October 7, but when Jones tried to do so, he was told to wait until October 10. On that day Jones was told once again that the apartment wasn't available. Angry and needing a place for his large family of ten, Jones ignored Coleman and moved in on October 11. The apartment was in terrible shape.

"I didn't have no lights, no water, no nothing," Albert Jones later testified. The toilets froze in the cold weather. Coleman made no repairs to the apartment, despite repeated demands by Jones. Frustrated, Jones decided to call the police, hoping they would do something. Two cops arrived in a squad car, went in, and looked around the basement as Jones explained that Coleman had taken his money and was not repairing anything. The cops shook their heads, told Jones that Coleman had fleeced him and the place "was awful," but did nothing else.

Coleman subsequently tried to lease the entire building to an Anthony Barnett, who paid him $425. Barnett soon discovered that Coleman had leased the basement to Jones and that Hickman had a claim against him for a hundred dollars, so he went to the police and had a warrant sworn out on him. Coleman began to fall behind on his own monthly payments to Adams at the same time. Where was all the money going?

Winter was fast approaching, and temperatures were dropping. Fires started breaking out across the city because of ill-maintained and dangerous heating systems. On November 19, a week before Thanksgiving, a small fire broke out in the rear end of the Washburne building's basement, dangerously close to Albert Jones's family. Everyone fled out into the cold as the Chicago Fire Department put out the blaze. No one was injured.

Afterward the whole building was inspected from top to bottom by fire officials on the scene. Chief Harry Nilson of the Chicago Fire Department's Fifteenth Battalion was shocked at the conditions he found throughout the building. He noted that there was no water or gas in the building and only "some electrical." Nilson walked up to the attic while the last of the smoke of the basement fire was still hanging in the air. He found three small rooms with furniture and clothing. Large families were obviously living in each of them. He went outside and asked how many people lived in the attic, and was told there were three families—seven persons in the back, eight in the center, and six (the Hickmans) in the front, for a total of twenty-one people. Nilson told all of them that this was too dangerous a place to live. After receiving this warning, two families moved out. The Hickmans, having no place to go, remained in the attic.

Nilson was a veteran firefighter and had seen many fires and needless deaths during his career. He sat down with Annie Hickman in her attic room and pointed to the window, telling her that in the event of another fire, she should climb out the window, hang there, and wait for a fire-department ladder. Nilson notified the city's building department and the fire prevention bureau of the unsafe conditions he had discovered.

The building department inspected 1733 West Washburne in early December 1946 and ordered Mary Adams to make repairs and remove trash, lumber, and other potentially combustible material from the premises. City building inspectors returned again a few weeks later and ordered Adams and Coleman to reduce the illegal overcrowding of many apartments, exterminate rats, and repair the plumbing. On December 27

David Coleman was served notice to correct seven code violations and to "place premises in habitable condition or vacate same." Coleman and Adams ignored the citations. There were no follow-up inspections by the building department, despite repeated complaints from the tenants that nothing had been fixed or replaced.

The new year brought no relief to the building's residents or to the thousands of other Chicagoans living in similar conditions. Black Chicago was in danger of burning down from landlord greed and neglect.

On January 12, a Sunday, another small fire broke out in the chimney of 1733 West Washburne. The fire department returned to put it out. Julia Rogers, the most vocal of the tenants, called Mary Adams to tell her about the fire and demand that she fix the broken water pipes. No one in the building had any running water.

"We all have children," Rogers told Adams, hoping that this might draw some sympathy from her. But Adams said this was "not her concern." Furious, Rogers told Adams that the tenants would fix the broken pipes themselves. Adams threatened to have them arrested. Elgin Rogers, Julia's husband, then got on the phone.

"Is there anything you can do for us?" he asked.

"Well, you all not paying enough rent here," Adams snapped. "I can rent this place for fifty dollars a month if I got you people out of there . . . instead of eleven dollars."

Rogers was filled with anger and contempt.

"I'm not going to fix anything," Adams told him. "Get out."

The fires made the remaining residents more fearful. It was a wonder that anyone could sleep at night. James Hickman confided to Annie that he was afraid "this building is liable to go down at any time." The threat David Coleman had made months earlier was still in his mind. Coleman and Adams had so far successfully avoided all efforts to make them comply with the most basic building, health, and safety codes, and no one seemed to be able to hold them accountable. The Hickmans were now the only family still living in the attic. The other two rooms were empty save for a bed frame and some clothes in the center room. The narrow wooden staircase connecting the third floor to the attic was the Hickmans' tenuous lifeline if they had to flee the building in an emergency.

Late at night while everyone slept, during the second week of January, Annie was awakened on three separate nights by the sound of someone slowly creeping up and down the stairs to the attic. She was too frightened to go out into the hall and see who it was. The stairs and the hall had no lighting, so whoever it was must have been sure of their footing. James was working the day shift that week from seven in the morning to three in the afternoon, and was at home at night.

"Didn't you hear somebody tipping up the stairs to the door and tipping down?" Annie asked James.

"I wonder what they are up to," James worried.

Then, revealing what he feared most, he asked her, "Do you reckon that somebody would burn us up here?"

To calm him down, she quickly said no.

To safeguard the family, Annie and James started having their eldest sons stay with them, especially when James was at work. Charles Hickman was nineteen and had been laid off from work since Christmas. Willis Hickman was working as a mail handler at the massive US Post Office at Van Buren and Canal Streets. The addition of the two older sons made the small room even more cramped, but it brought some comfort to Annie and the youngest children.

On the night of January 16, 1947, Willis didn't get to 1733 West Washburne until after 8:00 p.m.—he had stopped to get a haircut. He helped his youngest brothers and sisters with their school lessons. After James left for work that night, the rest of the family prepared for bed. They turned off the stove and the two lamps and locked the door. Annie and the youngest children accommodated themselves in one bed, Willis and Charles in the other. It was nearly 10:00 p.m.

Notified at 3:50 a.m.—several hours after the fire had overcome his four youngest children—that there was "trouble," James Hickman did not make it home until it was already light outside. When he tried to walk upstairs, police officers on the scene told him that he could not go up.

"Man, you tell me I can't go up there, what's the trouble? I am James Hickman. I live there."

The cops asked him what floor he lived on and told him that there had been a big fire in the attic. Hickman asked where his family was, and the officers said they didn't know. That was when a neighbor told him four of his children were dead. James immediately recalled Coleman's threat to burn them out. He began to pace back and forth and fell silent. Tears welled up in his eyes. The neighbor thought Hickman "looked pretty bad, like he was losing his mind."

"I would leave the job, and just ride, hunting for a place for my folks."

3

The Revolutionary

It was a cold Friday morning on January 17, 1947, when Mike Bartell left his apartment to walk a few blocks south to the corner newsstand. Every morning he bought a copy of each of Chicago's daily newspapers, and on Saturdays he would also pick up the *Chicago Defender*, scanning it along with the other papers in search of political issues to wrap his hands around. A recent spate of tenement fires had already taken a deadly toll on the South Side and had been extensively covered by the dailies. But nothing prepared him for the shocking front pages that morning.

The Daily Times' front page had two photographs of the gutted attic at 1733 West Washburne, one with firefighters sifting through the debris and another of the bed where the remains of the four Hickman children had been discovered. The caption read "Unsafe Attic—Home Burns; 4 Children Die." Scanning the inside pages, Bartell learned that two members of the Hickman family, Annie and Charles, had survived by jumping from the third floor. He grabbed a copy of the *Herald-American*. "Four More Die in Firetrap, 40 Others Routed" was its headline. "A firetrap

Negro tenement building at 1733 Washburne Ave. became the funeral pyre of four children early today," wrote the *Herald-American* reporter. Bartell paid for the papers, turned around, and quickly went back home.

Mike Bartell was born Milton Zaslow in New York City in 1918. (Radicals and trade unionists commonly used pseudonyms to protect themselves and their families from blacklisting by employers and landlords.) He was good-looking, with dark hair and eyes and a serious demeanor. Everyone who knew him said that he had a warm and attractive personality. His friend and protégé Frank Fried remembers that Mike "sparkled with confidence and was the best organizer I ever knew."

Bartell had become a Marxist in the early 1930s when the Great Depression, the rise of fascism, and the very beginnings of a combative workers' movement forced a whole generation to pick a side to fight on. "These were tumultuous times," Bartell told a group of student activists five decades later, trying to convey the excitement of the era.

Bartell became an active member of the Communist Party (CP)'s youth group, the Young Communist League (YCL), at the City College of New York (CCNY). In 1934, when he was as a freshman, the YCL had five units (branches) on campus, including a secret unit in ROTC (Reserve Officer Training Corps), which published a regular newspaper called *Red Cadet*. Bartell called the City College campus of the 1930s "the Berkeley of its time." It was one of the nationally recognized centers of student activism and radical politics; many City College activists went on to become prominent figures in the American left.

The major competition that the YCL faced on campus was the much smaller but politically aggressive group of supporters of the exiled Russian revolutionary Leon Trotsky, the "Trotskyites," as the YCLers called them derisively. Trotsky had been a key leader in the October Revolution and the commander of the Red Army during Russia's civil war. Later he became the leading opponent of the rising bureaucracy under Stalin that consolidated itself on the ruins of the workers' democracy Trotsky had fought to build. Starting in the mid-1920s, he had written hundreds of articles, letters, pamphlets, and books attacking the totalitarian leadership of the Soviet Union and Joseph Stalin's leadership of the international communist movement. The City College cafeteria was one of a handful of places where such issues were openly debated.

"The debate was permanent, " Bartell remembers, as partisans of both groups would come and go all day long. "It was very educational. It was through these debates that I began to have doubts about the YCL and became a Trotskyist." Bartell came under suspicion of being of a Trotsky sympathizer and was ordered to report to the CP's headquarters in Lower Manhattan. He met with former student leader Joseph Clark, who told him, "In the Soviet Union we would kill you. Here we can only expel you."

After he was expelled from the YCL, Bartell brought his restless energy to the Trotskyist movement. James Cannon and Max Shachtman, former founders and leaders of the American communist movement, became the key leaders of American Trotskyism. They had left the CP in 1928, supporting Trotsky over Stalin, and through the next decade they built a small revolutionary organization, the Communist League of America, with a talented group of writers, intellectuals, and trade union activists. League members were the leaders of one of the most important strikes of the 1930s, the Minneapolis Teamster strikes that prefaced the formation of the Congress of Industrial Organizations (CIO), the militant union movement of the era. American Trotskyists formed an independent nationwide political party in 1938, the Socialist Workers Party. Bartell was typical of many of the young people in the newly formed SWP, ambitious and charismatic, with good leadership skills.

The year before the SWP's formation, in June 1937, Bartell had his first serious run-in with the law while picketing a store in Brooklyn. He was accused of tossing a stink bomb through the store window that damaged $250 worth of clothing. After he was arrested, he told the cops that he was employed for two dollars per day by the union to picket the store. Eleven months later on March 17, 1938, he pleaded guilty to damaging property and was sentenced to the New York Reformatory. The sentence was suspended, however, and he was placed on probation. The more serious charge of throwing a stink bomb was dismissed.

During the Second World War the FBI opened up a file on Bartell, considering him a security risk. In an interview FBI agents conducted with Bartell's probation officer, he described Bartell "as [a] well educated, antisocial, maladjusted type, who has acquired Communistic ideas though educated at the city's expense."

Bartell left New York in 1939 to become the SWP's youth organizer in Los Angeles. But within a year of arriving, he decided that he wanted to get a job in the burgeoning aircraft or shipbuilding industry, where he could become a union activist. After being fired from a job at Lockheed Aviation in Burbank in 1941 for "radical activity" (according to his FBI file), he got a job at the Bethlehem Shipbuilding Corporation in San Pedro, the port district of Los Angeles, known for its busy waterfront of loading docks, canneries, and shipbuilding yards. Here he worked for nearly two years before he was laid off. He then worked as a longshoreman for about a year until he was hired as a machinist for the West Cost Shipbuilding Corporation. He quickly emerged as a leader and was elected a shop steward and then a member of the executive board of Local 9 of the CIO Industrial Union of Marine and Shipyard Workers. His workplace radicalism resulted in his being placed on the "key figure list" of the Los Angeles Field Division of the FBI.

During this time he met his future wife, Edith, a socialist and union activist in her own right. Born Edith Rose Bernstein on March 6, 1912, in New York City—the daughter of Russian Jewish immigrants—she was six years older than Bartell. She had moved to California with her first husband in the 1930s and opened a socialist bookstore in downtown Los Angeles.

In the two-year period from August 1939 to October 1941, she was arrested several times on picket lines for supporting striking workers. Most of the time she was charged and paid fines for violating city ordinances against picketing. In other cases, she was charged by the police with battery on scabs but had the charges dismissed or was fined.

Mike and Edith were married in October 1941. Their first and only child, Michael Joel Zaslow, known as Mickey to friends and family, was born on November 1, 1942, in Inglewood, California.

Bartell was twenty-three when the Japanese bombed Pearl Harbor and the United States fully entered the Second World War. He was of draft age but was initially given a draft deferment because he worked in a war industry. He was eventually declared 4-F—ineligible for military service—because of a childhood illness (osteomyelitis) that had left him with one leg shorter than the other.

In 1944, the national leadership of the SWP asked Bartell to leave California and take a full-time position as city organizer of the Chicago branch. It was not a welcome request. Bartell and his wife liked California. He had only lived there for a few years but had done well there.

What irked him even more was that the party asked him to leave for Chicago immediately, which meant leaving his wife and infant son behind. He discussed it with Edith, and they figured out how to do it. Both of them were dedicated members of the SWP, and Bartell could certainly make a mark for himself in the city that competed with New York as the capital of American radicalism. When Bartell arrived the SWP had around 150 members in the greater Chicago area, but it had lost many of its most promising young men to the draft. Edith and Mickey joined him in Chicago in early January 1945.

He arrived in Chicago on November 28, 1944. After receiving a tutorial on Chicago politics from the SWP's attorney, M. J. "Mike" Myer, and getting a feel for the membership, Bartell put forward some ambitious plans for the branch. Among them were tenant organizing and civil rights activism. Renters had a lot of grievances against their landlords, who used the wartime housing shortage to gouge their tenants. Black workers who were migrating to the city were particularly susceptible to landlord greed and neglect.

Edith took the lead by organizing a tenant union in the building where they lived at 4107 North Sheridan Road in Uptown, a mixed working- and middle-class neighborhood. The tenants' union put pressure on the OPA to keep rent prices stable and force landlords to improve living conditions in their buildings. Avaricious landlords showed their displeasure by refusing to repair or upgrade their properties. Everything was allowed to fall apart: roofs leaked, broken windows weren't replaced, and faulty wiring and broken water pipes were never repaired. The shortage of available housing kept renters from moving, and as a result, they saw their housing conditions deteriorate during and immediately after the war. This situation was even worse for Black renters, with fires frequently plaguing the tenements they occupied.

From the Bartells' building, tenant organizing spread throughout the North Side, and over the next two years it evolved into a citywide organization, the Chicago Tenants Union. SWP members, including the party's attorney, Myer, became well versed in the ins and outs of dealing with the rent-control division of the OPA. They also developed relationships with civil rights activists concerned with housing issues in the emerging Black communities on the West Side.

A renewed struggle for Black freedom and equality had begun in the 1930s, in many cases led or initiated by the Communist Party, from the Scottsboro Boys case to the interracial unionism of the CIO. The war years sharpened the contradiction between American Black soldiers and sailors' fighting allegedly for freedom and democracy abroad and being denied freedom at home. Millions of Black men and women served in the various branches of the military, and in even larger numbers in an array of industries that proved crucial to the victory of the United States and its allies in the Second World War.

However the largest and most influential nationwide organizations—the NAACP, the Communist Party, the Socialist Party, and the CIO—subordinated the struggle for civil rights to their support for the war effort. They would not do anything to combat racism that might lead to strikes or other militant actions and, in turn, would put unwanted pressure on the Roosevelt administration. This opened up a political space for newly formed and much smaller groups to take up the fight.

The Congress of Racial Equality (CORE) was one such group. Founded in 1942 at the University of Chicago, CORE took many of the tactics of the labor movement, such as sit-ins, and applied them to the struggle for civil rights. Its first target was the aptly named White City Skating Rink in April 1942. Though located in a predominantly Black neighborhood on the city's South Side, it denied access to Blacks or interracial couples. Despite militant picketing and a legal suit, White City successfully fought off CORE's challenge.

Undaunted, CORE moved on to two of Chicago's best-known restaurants, the Jack Spratt Coffeehouse, near the University of Chicago campus in Hyde Park, and Stoner's, in the Loop. Each had a long history of hostile and demeaning treatment of Black patrons. In May and June 1943, members of CORE and supporters sat in at both restaurants and caused such a commotion that the managers of both agreed to end their discriminatory policies.

With the war's end, Gerald Bullock, a young schoolteacher, was elected chairman of Chicago CORE and made a broad appeal for new members and activity. Mike Bartell responded enthusiastically to Bullock's call and suggested that activists take another crack at the notorious White City Skating Rink.

Beginning on the first Sunday in January 1946, weekly pickets converged on the rink. The pickets began modestly, with twenty or so people carrying banners and signs. The picket line was half Black and half white and made up mostly of members of the SWP and CORE. The police were called, and much to his surprise, rink manager Robert Michel was arrested for violating the city's civil rights ordinance. Mike Myer also filed suit in civil court on behalf of two CORE members who had been denied admission.

Pickets grew each week, with the largest being on the last Sunday in January 1946. That day a rally was first held at a nearby African Methodist Episcopal (AME) church, where Michael Mann, secretary of the Chicago CIO Industrial Union Council, pledged, "White City Skating Rink will be closed unless everyone is allowed to skate without regard to their color."

With that 150 people marched to the rink, including Mann, Bullock, Willoughby "Bill" Abner (vice president of the council and president of UAW Local 734), and Homer Jack of the Chicago Council on Religious and Racial Discrimination. Mike Bartell told the picketers that White City was "a symbol of the whole Jim Crow system which can only be wiped out by the united action of the workers and the Negro people."

Deprived of customers and soon after defeated in court, the rink's owner finally agreed to open White City to all the city's residents regardless of race. It was a small but important victory.

When Mike Bartell rushed into his apartment with the dailies, Edith was preparing breakfast for the family. Mike opened the newspapers and spread them out on the table. He and Edith discussed the Hickman fire and decided that it would be best for Mike to go immediately to the Chicago SWP office and start coordinating its response.

Bartell took the "L" and streetcars and got off near his office at 777 West Jackson, just a few blocks from Jane Addams's famed Hull House. The sun was beginning to illuminate the winter-gray city as he went into his office, made a pot of coffee, and again surveyed the newspaper accounts of the fire. It wasn't clear from these stories whether the building had been destroyed or made uninhabitable by water damage.

Nine months later, when he had a chance to sit down and collect his thoughts, he wrote to the SWP's national office in New York:

> I must tell you a little about our campaign against fire traps and unsanitary housing. This promises to be a most fruitful campaign. As you know, there had been three disastrous fires in within eight days, causing the death of 11 people. All were in Negro slums, the first two were on the south side and the third on the west side. The first two caught in the midst of our petition campaign [for public office], and we deemed it inadvisable to dump that once it had been started. The third took place on the west side. . . . We decided to jump into the situation, and the results were somewhat astounding.

Astounding was still to come on the morning of January 17 when he swung to action. Articles had to be written, public meetings had to be planned, contact had to be made with the surviving members of the Hickman family, and the remaining tenants at 1733 West Washburne needed to be organized. There was so much to do.

Cook County Hospital was an imposing structure on Chicago's West Side. Unkown to Bartell at the time, the police had whisked James Hickman away to this hospital to be reunited with his surviving family members. It was only half a mile away from 1733 West Washburne. With the fourteen elevated granite columns on the front of the building, it exuded authority like a courthouse, a city hall, or a bank. The once white granite had become gray over the years, giving the hospital a somber, almost ominous appearance. "County," as everyone called it, provided care for the city's working class on the North and West Sides. It was also home to the Cook County Morgue.

A distraught James Hickman was escorted to the rooms where he found his wife, Annie, with a broken leg, and his eldest son, Willis, who had a broken collarbone. Both were in casts and in deep pain. Charles was physically unscathed by the fire, but he had endured the excruciating task of identifying his youngest siblings hours before at the coroner's office.

Dr. J. J. Kearns, chief pathologist for the coroner's office, had performed autopsies on the Hickman children. He had been chief pathologist since 1932; a brief brush with fame had come in 1934, when he performed an autopsy on John Dillinger, the infamous "Public Enemy Number 1," after he was gunned down by FBI agents outside the Biograph Theater on Lincoln Street on the city's North Side.

Kearns wrote detailed notes of his examination:

Lester Hickman: 14 years old, 5 feet, 5 inches, 75 pounds.
Elzana [*sic*] Hickman: 9 years old, 4 feet, 9 inches, 65 pounds.
Sylvester Hickman: 7 years old, 5 feet, 60 pounds.
Velvana [*sic*] Hickman: 4 [3] years, 3 feet, 10 inches, 40 pounds.

Each of the bodies had burns and smoke damage from the inferno that had engulfed the tiny attic room. "The skin of the head, neck, trunk and extremities is superficially absent exposing a pinkish red surface, or, vesiculated," wrote Kearns. "The mucosa of the lips, tongue and buccal cavity is swollen and discolored dark gray to grayish black." He concluded that the cause of death of all the Hickman children "was extensive second degree burns." James Hickman signed the official forms identifying his youngest children and those necessary to release their bodies to a funeral home. As they reeled under the enormity of their loss, the private struggles and pain of the Hickman family were about to come into public view.

"Paper was made to burn, coal and rags, not people. People wasn't made to burn."

4

"Trapped like rats"

The Cook County Coroner's Office conducted the first official investigation into the deaths of the Hickman children. At the time the coroner was an elected official in each Illinois county, and his office impaneled a jury to investigate the cause of any suspicious death and forward its findings to the state's attorney. The inquests were public hearings, and anyone could attend. The coroner and deputy coroners didn't perform autopsies; they were administrators. Their medical staff conducted the examinations.

Alexander Lewis Brodie, known as "A. L.," was coroner of Cook County in 1947. He had first been appointed to the office in February 1940 and was elected coroner the following December. Brodie had been born and raised in Chicago and was a lifelong Democrat. He rose to become vice president of the National Coroners' Association and was author of the *Coroner's Manual.* The coroner's office couldn't prosecute anyone, but his office was the first to deal with any suspicious deaths ranging from house fires to gangland killings to major accidents, and had the power to subpoena witnesses. This gave Brodie a significant political role in the city. It also meant that his office was subject to enormous political pressure, particularly from city hall.

Bartell called Mike Myer at his office and filled him in on the day's events. Myer told him it was likely that a coroner's inquest would be held that day at the morgue or at the Cook County building in the Loop. They agreed that it was important to meet with James Hickman as soon as the first hearing was over in order to get a campaign off and running. The hearing was scheduled for 2:30 p.m. on January 17—just seven hours after Hickman discovered the "trouble" that had devastated his family.

It was a moment of high drama—four dead children, front-page news stories, political leaders outraged, demands for action—when A. L. Brodie called to order his "Inquest on the bodies of Sylvester Hickman, Velvana Hickman, Elzana Hickman and Lester Hickman." (The coroner's office had misspelled the names of Elzina and Velvina.) Also present were Earl Downes, the city's assistant corporation counsel representing the fire department, and Deputy Coroner Eugene Ingles. Conspicuously absent were David Coleman and Mary Adams.

The first to testify was Chief Harry Nilson. He recounted his many visits to 1733 West Washburne and the conditions he had found there, and then he got to the fire. It started in the middle room of the attic, he said, where his men found a burned-up bed, which seemed to be the only furniture in the room. However, "as far as determining just what started it, I could not tell at this time."

"What type of heating did they use?" asked Downes.

"They had a small kerosene stove in their flat that was set out, but that had been turned off and that was out, and they had retired for the night and apparently they had put it out, because there was no fire in the stove."

Nilson was sure that the fire didn't start in the Hickman family room, and he was sure that the fire wasn't the result of anything the Hickmans did.

Next to testify was Sergeant Arthur Madzinski, one of the first policemen at the scene of the fire. Brodie pressed Madzinski with questions about the Hickmans' stove and got confirmation that the stove was not responsible for the fire.

Brodie sensed that there was something seriously wrong with the picture that Nilson and Madzinski were painting of the fire. "Well, it seems strange that the stove was out and yet there was a fire, a fire serious enough to kill four people." His anger boiled over: "Four children, *trapped like rats in a little hole up there.*"

His office had presided over too many hearings recently regarding children who had died in unsafe housing.

Nilson jumped back in.

"Mr. Coroner, that stove that they had was upright when I got there, and if it was in that position, it was not that stove started the fire, and *that was the only stove in the attic.*"

Charles Hickman was the first of the surviving family members to testify (as Annie and Willis Hickman were hospitalized, they could not appear). The harrowing events of the last eighteen hours must have left Charles in a state of physical exhaustion and mental shock. He recounted being woken up by his mother and noted that the fire had started in the center room, but he didn't know what caused it.

Brodie probed further about the center room. "Did you keep any gasoline in that room, or kerosene?"

"We kept kerosene in our room to heat up the oil burner."

"That is in your room, where you live?"

"That is right."

"Did you keep any gasoline in the other room—was there?"

"No."

"There was some kerosene in about the center of the attic but that was not of a high flash point that would have any bearing on that fire, *unless someone had ignited it,*" Nilson interjected.

Nilson then asked if Charles remembered seeing a can of kerosene on the east side of the center room of the attic.

"Yes."

The questions hanging in the air were why a can of kerosene was in the center room and, more important, who put it there?

When James Hickman took the stand, all eyes were on him, the aggrieved father who had just lost four young children and nearly lost his wife and two eldest sons. His pain must have been unbearable, but his testimony was straightforward and to the point. Under the circumstances his testimony is remarkable for its restraint.

He recounted how he had come to live at 1733 West Washburne and his frustrating dealings with David Coleman. He was adamant that the stove in the family's room was not the cause of the deadly fire. When Brodie asked whether he knew how the fire started, he replied, "I sure don't, but it was no way possible for the heater to catch; there is no pipe, no way for sparks. We had a Kenmore, two burner stove, and no way for nothing to explode."

Brodie asked him if it were possible that the kerosene lamps used to light the room could have fallen and caused the fire.

"It could not," James insisted. "We had been mighty particular with everything for twenty-three years that me and my wife had been married. We was careless with nothing. Even the children, not careless even with matches, even to strike them for a cigarette."

"Do you feel anybody might have set your place on fire?" Brodie asked.

"I wouldn't go to say anybody must have set it on fire. I might accuse somebody wrong, but, by the way, it didn't set itself."

Why didn't Hickman tell them that Coleman had threatened to burn him out the previous September? A clue might be found in his words "I might accuse somebody wrong." James had lived almost his entire life in Mississippi, where Black men were frequently lynched after being falsely accused of crimes from rape to theft. This may have made him reticent to recount Coleman's threat. If Brodie had put his question slightly differently, asking, say, "Did anyone ever threaten you and your family?" he might have gotten a different answer.

Earl Downes then asked James whether someone could access the attic's center room without going through the room the Hickmans lived in. James told him yes. All that was required to get into the center room of the attic was a key to the building; once inside, a person could readily enter the attic. If you had a rough idea of when the building's residents were likely to be at work or sleeping, you could get access to the attic and avoid being seen.

When Annie and James heard someone tiptoeing up and down the stairs, was this someone a burglar, a curious neighbor—or an arsonist? This question was not posed openly at the inquest.

Brodie's anger boiled over again at the atrocious picture being painted of living conditions at 1733 West Washburne:

> If some of the landlords were pushed around a little and given to under-
> stand they are renting to human beings, they would be probably a little
> more careful; and I do believe that the proper agencies should know things
> of this sort are going on. These fellows buy without inspecting and try to
> milk the building dry as they can, irrespective of the security of the people
> they are renting to. I believe some of those fellows belong behind bars. I
> think it is a crime. I think that man is just as guilty as fire itself, in the de-
> struction of these human lives. It is too bad there isn't a law to throw them
> in jail.

Was Brodie grandstanding for the public, genuinely outraged, or both? His public tongue-lashing of the landlords gave Julia Rogers confidence to present the most explosive testimony of the day. She described the horrid conditions in the building and her troubled dealings with Mary Adams. But it was with the arrival of Coleman in July 1946, she said, that things took an ominous turn. Rogers told the coroner and the jury that after Coleman failed to push out the tenants, he told her "he would go to the length, if it had to be a fire."

Brodie was shocked. "Coleman said that?" This was potentially a major breakthrough in the inquest. "I will ask the police to bring Mr. Coleman in to question him along those lines."

Rogers proceeded to reveal Adams's callous attitude toward the safety of the children in the building, especially after the fire in the chimney.

"She said that the children wasn't her concern. So, I don't know what she is going to think now, because it could have been mine just like it was Mrs. Hickman's."

Brodie decreed that Mary Adams also must appear at the next hearing.

Rogers finished her testimony and was excused. What had begun as an inquest into a tragic house fire was now escalating into a very public investigation of unsafe housing, a failure of government oversight, and possibly arson and homicide.

"I would like to ask the police department, the fire department, Corporation Counsel's office to notify any civic agency who wants to come along and help in this thing. Let's have a complete and thorough investigation," Brodie said, "not only of the fire, but these deplorable conditions existing in these poor tenement homes. I don't think there should be such a thing as underprivileged people. I think a person should be privileged to live and enjoy life."

He adjourned the hearing. It would reconvene in three weeks, on February 7.

Soon after the first hearing into the death of the Hickman children was adjourned, several members of the SWP who lived on the West Side—Mike Bartell called them "our West Side group"—met with James Hickman. They explained that they wanted to organize several meetings to support the Hickman family and publicize the terrible conditions that were leading to so many unnecessary deaths. They also wanted Hickman to have the best possible legal counsel and encouraged him to consider Mike Myer, an experienced housing attorney, to represent him and his family. They asked Hickman if he would speak at the meetings, and surprisingly, given how little time has passed since the deadly fire, Hickman agreed to do so.

This wasn't the first time Bartell had taken the initiative in a very difficult situation with little information and no direct connection to the people involved. The previous year he had investigated a story about an African American woman, Grace Hardy, who had moved into a previously all-white neighborhood on the 300 block of West Garfield on the South Side. Her home had been firebombed and badly damaged. She barely survived, with severe burns that had kept her in the hospital from May 1 through early August 1946. The police did nothing to find the arsonists, and the big daily newspapers had ignored the case. Bartell traced Hardy to the hospital and interviewed her, photographing her sitting up with her right arm completely wrapped in bandages. He then organized a delegation of ten civil rights and labor organizations—including members of CORE, the NAACP, the CIO, the Urban League, and the SWP—that confronted Chicago police chief John Prendergast with what the *Chicago Defender* called "a scathing criticism of police failure to apprehend vandals guilty of 27 bombings of Negro homes in restrictive covenant areas."

The delegation had acted, the *Defender* reported, "after receiving reports of a six-week-old plot by local authorities to suppress circumstances of the incendiary bombing of the home of Mrs. Grace Hardy." Prendergast pledged action, but nothing came of it. No one was ever prosecuted. A "Grace Hardy Fund" was created, however, to help her make payments on her house and repair the damage done by the bombing.

Bartell hoped to do better for the Hickman family. He organized a delegation of SWP members, and with the help of the residents of 1733 West Washburne, they inspected the building from top to bottom on Saturday January 18. Bartell led the delegation as they examined the charred remnants of the attic and the rest of the building, including the partially flooded basement where the Albert Jones family lived. Bartell thought that the conditions were "shocking." The horrid conditions that led to the deaths of the Hickman children were only rivaled by what he and the others discovered in the basement, which "was rented to a family of ten at $300 in advance and $50.00 a month, also with no facilities, but plenty of rats, and floors which were constantly flooded by broken pipes. Constant appeals to the board of health had been futile."

On Sunday morning, 1733 West Washburne tenants attended a meeting called by the SWP where Bartell laid out the case for solidifying the tenants' union they had formed the morning after the fire. Mike Myer discussed the tenants' legal rights and agreed to represent them in their legal battle with their landlord. He also announced that the Hickman family had retained him in a civil suit against Mary Adams for the death of their children. The tenants drew up a list of demands, including demands for fire escapes and fire extinguishers in every apartment and the restoration of electrical, water, and gas service. They voted to continue the rent strike they had begun two days earlier until they won, and to organize a mass public meeting the next night.

"No More Fire Victims!" was the headline on the flyer advertising the meeting. Reverend V. B. Watts hosted it at his Progressive Baptist Church on the city's West Side. The meeting voted to create a West Side Tenants Union, organized around three demands on the city: (1) add firemen, equipment, and more fire escapes in dangerous areas; (2) construct emergency housing for tenants of unsafe buildings; and (3) abolish restrictive covenants and initiate a construction program to build low-cost housing.

"Despite near-zero weather the meeting was jammed. The West Side Tenants Union was established and the proposed three-point program unanimously adopted. A temporary executive committee of ten was elected," wrote Robert Birchman, a member of the SWP in Chicago and a prolific writer for the SWP's newspaper, *The Militant*, and its magazine, the *Fourth International*. Birchman had been a founding member of the SWP in 1938 and had been writing about racism and housing in Chicago for years.

James Hickman and Julia Rogers both addressed the meeting. Rogers told the audience, "Only by sticking together can we get anything. When you speak to the landlords about fixing things they do nothing. Landlords just take your rent. They don't care."

Mike Myer asked the crowd to think about the larger goals that they were fighting for: "You are here not just because four children are dead, tragic as that is. You are here to prevent any recurrence of these tragic fires and the loss of lives. Even if someone goes to jail for being responsible for the fire that killed the Hickman children, that does not solve the problem. The authorities don't want to tackle the problem. You must act as one to see that conditions are improved." Myer so impressed the audience that they asked him, and he agreed, to represent them during the coroner's inquest and in a suit against their landlord.

Reverend Watts wrapped up the meeting by exhorting the crowd: "We do not look upon this as a racial issue. We want protection regardless of the color of the landlord. Some of our folks when they get money just step in our faces. Let us look at what the landlords are doing. Don't be Uncle Toms! Get the union organized!" A hat was passed and more than one hundred dollars was raised for the Hickman family.

Mike Bartell didn't know it at the time, but he had taken the first steps in organizing the most important political campaign of his life.

"It seems like I can see a future for you."

5
"This can happen to you"

The Wesley Chapel on Maxwell Street overflowed with mourners. At the front, the Hickman children's caskets, draped in white cloth, were arranged by age and size from left to right. Lester, who had used his body to shield his siblings, had the largest casket. Beside him were the caskets for the bodies of Velvina, Sylvester, and the youngest, Elzina. The minister presided just to the left of the caskets, while a choir sang hymns on the right. The surviving members of the Hickman family sat in the front row, with the exception of Annie, who was still hospitalized because of her injuries from the fire. A distraught James Hickman sat with his eyes downcast; a female parishioner laid her hand on his left shoulder to comfort him.

The children were buried at Restvale Cemetery in the far south suburb of Alsip, nearly twenty miles from the chapel. African Americans found it virtually impossible to bury their family members in the cemeteries of Chicago proper, because of the racism deeply ingrained in the practices of most cemetery associations.

The *Chicago Defender* reporter assigned to the Hickman funeral looked at the four small coffins and was reminded of a "similar occasion the week before when rites were held for other children burned to death in a fire at 31st Street and Cottage Grove Avenue." They were the four young children of Clarence and Bessie Mae White, who, the *Defender* reported, did "not even have pictures of their children as mementos. Everything they had was lost in the fire." The *Defender* warned its readers: "This can happen to you."

The White family had been living in a small four-room apartment in the rear of a block-long four-story building on the South Side of Chicago. The building had once been a luxury hotel built to house visitors to the Chicago World's Fair of 1893, but now it housed more than five hundred people and a Baptist church. Clarence and Bessie Mae White had been living in the city with their four young children for less than three years when tragedy struck. On the afternoon of January 9, 1947, around 3:15 p.m., Bessie Mae heard "a noise, like a noise of cracking," while she was on her knees scrubbing the floor. She looked up and saw a "blaze and smoke was coming down" from the ceiling. The ceiling and walls of her apartment began to collapse. She ran out of her apartment and yelled: "Fire!" The wind slammed the door shut and locked behind her.

"I broke the door with my foot and my fist, and at the time I had the door open, my oldest boy was getting burned to death, he was crawling around on the floor." She picked up her eldest son, Clarence Jr., whose clothes were on fire. "I took him out, and some gentleman around took him away from me."

The gentleman was forty-four-year-old Earl Thompson, a Black truck driver for R.R. Donnelley, one of the largest printers in Chicago. Thompson reported, "I was standing on the corner, at the southeast corner. I don't know the approximate time when an elderly gentleman came up to me and said it was a fire there, and kids in the building." He ran to the back of the alley and saw fire coming out of the building. "I heard some noise on the first floor, and knew it was children in there."

Thompson saw Bessie with one of her children in her arms. "He was badly burned, and I smother the fire and smoke with my overcoat while she tried to get the other ones." A Bell Telephone repairman—working in a nearby alley—told Thompson to get in his truck with the boy, and they headed for Michael Reese Hospital. Thompson left his name and telephone number with the hospital staff in case the police or the fire department needed to talk to him. He had to go to work.

Bessie White tried to get back into her apartment to save the rest of her children, but a fireman "would not let me go back into my house. All that I could do was stand outside and watch the fire, hoping for the safety of my children." The interior of the building was quickly being destroyed, but firemen helped thirty people escape the flames by climbing down ladders from their apartment windows. Three explosions rocked the fifty-year-old building, hampering rescue efforts as seventy-five uniformed police officers prevented tenants from trying to reenter to search for relatives or personal belongings.

The massive amounts of water used to fight the fire flooded the basement. As dusk approached on that wintry day, frozen water encased the ruins of the building. More than five hundred people, nearly two hundred families, were made homeless by the Cottage Grove fire. The White family suffered the greatest casualties, with the deaths of their four children: Clarence Jr. (age six), Magnolia (five), Walter (three), and Vernola, who was just six days short of her second birthday.

Clarence and Bessie Mae White lost literally everything in the fire. The *Defender* issued an appeal for "food, money, furniture and clothing" for the Whites and called on businesses and churches to donate their services for the proper care and burial of their children. Reverend Louis Henry Ford offered his St. Paul's Church of God in Christ for the funeral service. Morticians and funeral home companies furnished embalming, while others provided caskets, clothing, and other necessities. Cars for the burial procession were donated by several livery companies. Marjorie Stewart Joyner, director of the *Chicago Defender* Charities, assisted Reverend Ford with the details of the burial service.

The White family tragedy unnerved Chicago's Black community. The gruesomeness of little Walter's death in particular—90 percent of his body was covered with third-degree burns after the burning ceiling collapsed on him—highlighted the shoddy conditions in which many Blacks lived and the threat of dangerous fires hanging over them.

The tragedy could have slipped into obscurity had not all of the White children been members of the *Chicago Defender*'s Bud Billiken Club. "They never had a chance. They all died like rats," wrote an angry *Defender* editorial writer. "Stirred by the recent tragic deaths of four Billikens in the fire at 31st and Cottage Grove and the three adult victims of the blaze at 2944 Prairie Ave., Monday, the Chicago Defender Bud Billiken club, headed by David Kellum, ol' Bud Billiken himself, immediately adopted measures to prevent future recurrence of these tragedies."

Bud Billiken was a fictional character created by the *Defender*'s founder and publisher Robert S. Abbott, who had decided in 1923 that there should be a youth section in the paper. "The reason was twofold," according to Abbott's biographer, Roi Ottley: "[Abbott] was probing for a method by which he could enlist newsboys and maintain their interest in the paper; and he felt the paper needed reading matter of interest to young people in general." Newsboys sold the paper on street corners. They tended to be very young—preteen—and were an important means of getting the *Defender* out in Black neighborhoods. Abbott discussed his idea with Lucius C. Harper, the paper's news editor, who liked it.

While Abbott was talking to Harper, he noticed a squat Chinese-looking figurine on his desk. Harper told him it was a Chinese god called a *billiken*, a protector of children. It captured Abbott's imagination. After some brainstorming, Harper and Abbott decided that the young people's page editor should be called Bud Billiken. They wanted the editor to be a young person.

The first Bud Billiken was Willard Motley. Born in 1909 and raised in the Englewood neighborhood on Chicago's South Side, he came to Abbott's attention because of the literary talent he exhibited at a young age. Motley later wrote the best-selling novel *Knock on Any Door*. Abbott dressed Motley up in the costume of a newspaper editor of the time, with "horn-rimmed glasses and an editor's eye shade," and his picture in this getup appeared in every issue of the *Defender Junior,* a section of the regular *Defender.* Its masthead proclaimed it to be the "Children's Greatest Newspaper." It was filled with cartoons, jokes, puzzles, and morality tales. A Bud Billiken Club was formed in 1924, with membership cards and buttons distributed free. Letters from Billiken "pen pals" were printed. The section was immensely popular. The *Defender* started receiving a deluge of letters, some coming from as far away as Africa.

After Willard Motley served as Bud Billiken for two years, the mantle was passed to David W. Kellum. Born in 1903 in Greenville, Mississippi, Kellum had come to Chicago as a young boy. He was the first African American to be commissioned a major in the Reserve Officer Training Corps (ROTC) in Illinois. He remained as Bud Billiken for twenty-five years and helped turn it into an institution among Black children. The Bud Billiken Club grew to nearly one million members across the country.

In 1929, Abbott and Kellum approached several city officials about having an annual "Bud Billiken Day and Parade." The purpose of the parade would be to "give underprivileged children, who are never seen or heard, a chance to be in the limelight for one day by wearing costumes, marching in a parade, and being seen." Abbott led the parade in his limousine, followed by *Defender* newsboys and a procession of contingents and floats.

The parade became a South Side institution. There were years when the Young Communist League had a contingent. World heavyweight boxing champion Joe Louis was an honored guest. In 1945, the parade honored returned Black veterans ("Hail Our Conquering Heroes") of the Second World War with floats bearing enormous *V*s for victory. Mayor Ed Kelly proclaimed August 11, 1945, Bud Billiken Day and "urge[d] all citizens of Chicago to join in this great tribute to our children and to our heroes."

In response to the fire crisis, the Bud Billiken Club organized a "junior fire patrol." Launched with the slogan "Be Careful with Fire and

Save a Life," it was open to all school-age children. Kellum worked in cooperation with Police Chief Pendergrast and Fire Chief Anthony Mullaney. Kellum took to the radio on WGES, the Black-owned station, and visited schools to promote fire safety in the home. The goal was to try to involve fifty thousand school-age children in the Bud Billiken Junior Fire Patrol.

At the Doolittle Elementary School, 898 students pledged to join the fire patrol, and they collected over one thousand canned goods for the city's fire victims. St. Paul's Church of God in Christ graduated a class of one hundred for the fire patrol on February 9. The Junior Fire Patrol had fire wardens, block captains, and junior firefighters. David Kellum reminded students, "Fires know no color line and when disaster strikes it strikes whites as well as Negroes and we want you to know that your gift today will be distributed to all the poverty-stricken regardless of their race, color or religion." Kellum also issued Bud Billiken's Fire Safety Rules:

P—put out lighted matches and cigarettes. Never throw them away when lighted.

R—replace worn and frayed electric cords.

E—eliminate unnecessary accumulations of rubbish.

V—vertical openings in buildings must be cut off to prevent the spread of fire.

E—educate school children in simple rules of fire prevention.

N—never smoke in bed.

T—train every man, woman and child in what to do when fire endangers life or property.

F—flameproof decorations in all public places.

I—inspect all places where fire may occur frequently.

R—replace wooden shingled roofs with fire-retardant roof covering.

E—examine and maintain all fire appliances.

S—safeguard all heating equipment and appliances from surrounding combustible material.

The latest round of tenement fires had devastated Chicago's Black community. Eleven lives, including eight children, had been lost in seven days. Would these needless deaths shake the city's establishment into action? Were the fires an omen of a bigger conflagration? Some thought so. The *Chicago Daily News* warned that "Chicago is in danger of a great fire like the 1871 disaster that swept the city, alarmed officials warned today as another tenement blaze killed four children . . . Attention was focused on the South Side Negro district as the danger center. And the officials said: 'Something must be done, and quickly.'"

The bulk of the black population still lived in the narrow, overcrowded ghetto on the South Side. "There is a ghastly situation here," Dorothy Rubel, acting director of the Metropolitan Housing Council, told the *Chicago Daily News*. "The Chicago Negro district is the worst example of crowded housing in the metropolitan area." Municipal Judge Wendell E. Green was unnerved by the prospect that "there will be a blaze that will sweep the city. I fear the fire situation here will astound the nation."

Such newspaper stories discussed housing problems in the Black community as a threat to Chicago as a whole. But as the *Defender* forcefully argued, the problems were primarily confined to the city's Black neighborhoods and called for immediate political action. *Defender* publisher John H. Sengstacke, in a front-page editorial headlined "Mobilize to Halt Fire," wrote, "There can be no doubt that death lurks in every kitchenette and unprotected building. As a result of this deplorable condition, men, women, and children become helpless victims when caught . . . Chicago's Southside is a tinderbox, and every resident of the area is in greater danger of losing his life and home in flames than ever in the city's history."

Since November 1946 there had been 751 fires between Twenty-Sixth to Fifty-Ninth Streets, from Halsted to the Lake Michigan shoreline, the heart of Black Chicago. "Two things are needed," declared Sengstacke: "removal of the residential restrictions based on race and new housing." He called for a summit of Black community leaders to deal with the crisis. Housing had been at the top of the *Defender*'s agenda for many decades, and its editors had sent its reporters straight to the front line of Chicago's housing wars. Some barely survived to write about it.

Vernon Jarrett was one of the *Defender*'s young, talented, and fearless reporters. He believed that journalism was a special calling, especially for a young Black man: "To me, journalism is a vehicle for taking a stand and doing the most good for our race." Jarrett had been born in Paris, Tennessee, in 1918, the son of black schoolteachers. "My grandfather was a teenage runaway slave in the Civil War, but he was so illiterate he didn't know where he was from," Jarrett recalled many decades later. "He used to make my brother read the *Chicago Defender* out loud from cover to cover. I was too young to read, so I just sat back and enjoyed it. We didn't know until after he died that my grandfather couldn't read." Jarrett served in the army during the Second World War, and after graduating from college he moved to Chicago in 1946 to pursue a career in journalism at the *Defender*. "When I moved to Chicago and started working for the *Defender* in 1946, my first story was covering a race riot at the Airport Homes project, where a mob tried to kill some Black veterans." Jarrett neglected to mention that in the process he was almost killed.

Airport Homes was a housing complex that had been built during the Second World War on the South Side. It was a large complex of two-story duplexes that spanned several blocks. After the war, the federal government turned over the property to the Chicago Housing Authority (CHA). CHA director Elizabeth Wood, a well-known opponent of racial segregation in housing, announced that Airport Homes would be open to veterans regardless of race. Mayor Ed Kelly, who had appointed Wood to her position, was dumped as the Democratic Party's mayoral candidate in 1947 in part because of her policies.

One of the first veterans to register for housing at Airport Homes was Theodore Turner, an African American who had lost several ribs during the invasion of Anzio, the Italian coastal city that witnessed one of the most prolonged battles of the Second World War. Anticipating trouble, Turner turned to the United Negro and Allied Veterans of America

(UNAVA), a national grouping of mostly Black veterans created by members of the Communist Party. Jarrett accompanied the UNAVA, white veterans, union activists, and other supporters of Turner when he moved into his apartment with his family in late November 1946.

"A mob gathered and chased the veterans and the journalists, white and Black, up to the second floor of the duplex," Jarrett remembered.

"They had their little kids with them and they was chanting, 'Niggers go home! Niggers go home!' They tried to set fire to the building. One Black veteran got on the phone and called the police station. He said, 'You got some cops standing around out here chatting with these people. They're trying to kill us, and it's getting dark!'"

Jarrett was furious at the mob and thought they were little better than the Nazis who had just been defeated. He wrote at the time, "Displaying the raw ingredients of fascism, a frenzied mob of 200 whites—some shouting, 'Hitler was right'—laid siege to Negro and white sympathetic veterans here last week."

Two CHA officials sent to facilitate Turner's move-in, William Graham and Emil Hirsch, were chased away by the mob after their car was turned over by eight men. Facing what he thought was certain death, Turner got on the phone, called the police, and told them, "I'm going to my car to get my switchblade. If you don't have these cops give me some protection, somebody's going to get hurt."

Jarrett remembers that a few minutes later, "the cops standing with the mob came up and let us through. They escorted us to our cars because they thought that veteran would really kill someone."

The mob rocked Jarrett's car back and forth to try to turn it over but failed. Then they smashed all the windows with baseball bats. Jarrett and others were facing danger, but they were undeterred.

"It was a funny thing," Jarrett explained. "All of us brothers were out there, we were ready to fight. The Black veteran whose story I was covering had been in Italy so long he spoke conversational Italian. He came out of the car, ripped open his shirt, and pointed to his scars: 'This happened in Anzio!' Then he said it in Italian." One of the leaders of the mob was Italian American and was visibly startled by this, and the white veterans seemed to have been shamed and halted their attack.

The events of that day never left Jarrett, but for the vast majority of Chicagoans the mob action was not front-page news. The *Chicago Tribune*, for example, buried it on page 11, while the *Daily News* and the *Sun* published small page 3 stories. "The white newspapers had an agreement with the Mayor's Commission on Human Rights: They would treat this story as though it never happened. The *Defender* was the only one that ran the story [on its front page]. The editors suggested our bylines not appear on most stories, but I didn't give a damn—I was trying to change the world."

The second coroner's hearing into the death of the Hickman children was scheduled for February 7—three days after the death of the White children was ruled an "accident" (though the conditions that led to the death were condemned).

David Coleman had dodged the Chicago police for several weeks before he was finally arrested. He was brought into felony court and charged with larceny. Irving Lang, assistant state's attorney, charged that Coleman took twenty-five dollars from Nonie Bullitt, an African American resident of the South Side, on the promise that he would find her an apartment. He never did, nor did he return her money. Lang asked for a high bond for Coleman until the investigation into the fire at 1733 West Washburne was completed. Arson was suspected, and Julia Rogers had testified at the first coroner's hearing that Coleman had threatened to burn the residents out of his building. Despite this, Judge Charles S. Dougherty set Coleman free on fifty-dollar bail and his promise to appear at the coroner's hearing scheduled for a week later.

If other residents of 1733 West Washburne could substantiate the threat that Coleman had allegedly made to Rogers, he could be facing an investigation into arson and possibly murder. Mary Adams was clearly a callous, greedy property owner who let her tenants live in conditions unfit for human beings; but was she aware of Coleman's threat to burn her tenants out? Everything seemed set for a full hearing of the issues, but when Deputy Coroner Eugene Ingles called the hearing to order, there was an immediate problem.

"Have the record show," Ingles told the hearing reporter, "that we have had a hearing on this matter on the sixteenth day [he meant the seventeenth] of January, and it was continued at the time for further investigation by the police department." He called to the stand Sergeant Arthur Madzinski and reminded him that he still was under oath.

Madzinski had to explain why Coleman wasn't present to testify. "He was taken to the State's Attorney's office Monday, to the Assistant State's Attorney Irving Lang, who talked to him, had in Felony Court, had the case continued . . . with the understanding that he would be here today. I guess he is in Cook County jail now, I am sure here to make that report, his bond was set pretty high."

Madzinski wasn't aware that Coleman had been released from custody. Could this be a case of two agencies getting their wires crossed, or it could be a sign of a deeper problem with the police and the State's Attorney's Office? Didn't Lang inform Judge Dougherty that Coleman had been publicly accused of threatening arson shortly before the fire that killed the Hickman children? If he did, why did the judge release him on the basis of a promise to appear before the coroner? Mary Adams was also not present at the hearing, despite the earlier stipulation by A. L. Brodie. Ingles seemed resigned to the situation and announced that there would be a third hearing. "Well, they are not present today, and in view of that fact, we will have to continue the case so that all the witnesses we want will be present."

Ingles called to the stand the still-recovering Annie Hickman, who had broken one of her legs in the fall from the building and was still in great pain. Annie's testimony would have a powerful effect on the jury; she had struggled to raise four young children in very difficult circumstances and lost them in seconds just an arm's length away from her.

When asked about the living conditions at 1733 West Washburne, she replied in a matter-of-fact way: "It had none, no water, had no bath room, no lights, just plain lamp light, had no electricity, had to get water from the third floor, third floor to the toilet." Since Annie was the only survivor who could give an account of the fire from the moment of its discovery, her testimony would carry great weight.

She told of the night of the fire—her waking up to the strange sounds of the fire crackling, waking her children, and her dramatic escape from the burning building. Ingles asked her how quickly she reacted when she first heard the crackling of the flames. "I did not lie there a second, the second when I looked up, because when we woke before, the smoke was in my room at that time. The room, it got very hot, it was on a night, cold out there . . . it was so hot, and smoke was in the room and fire getting all around."

Annie's description of her escape dumbfounded Ingles, Chief Nilson, and members of the jury. They just couldn't wrap their heads around it. Nilson, who had witnessed countless fires, deaths, and near deaths during his career, was especially taken aback.

"Well, we don't want to spend any time on this," Nilson said to Ingles, "but, it is just a miracle she got down. I cannot quite seem to understand— well, I do now—just how she escaped. Can't quite understand—we were at the scene, Mr. Coroner, and if you could see the situation, you would wonder as we do. It was a miracle."

Ingles, equally mystified, simply replied, "The Lord was with her."

Nilson then returned to questioning her about the possible origins of the fire, specifically the kerosene-fueled stove and lamps. "That stove was out, didn't have any fire in it on that night, is that true?"

"Yes."

"It was stone cold when we got there?"

"That's right."

"That made the flat very cool."

"Surely."

"It was no fire in that little stove, is that right?"

"Yes."

"What about the lamps?" asked Ingles.

"Lamps was out."

"The lamps were out when you retired to bed?"

"Sure."

The key surviving witness had testified that the fire began outside the Hickmans' room. She went on to tell the jury that she had no direct dealings with Coleman about conditions in the building and that her husband, James, had tried to talk to him, but to no avail. Annie had learned of Coleman's threat to burn them out from her husband, not from Coleman himself.

"As far as you know," Ingles asked her, "who owns the building?"

"Well, when we went there, Coleman told us he had leased the building for one year. After we were there for a while, he said he had bought the building. He had taken over the building—well and another man, Mr. Barnett, later was then running it, he leased the building for five years, and he came there a few times."

"Who did you pay rent to?"

"To Mr. Coleman," Annie replied.

There appeared to be many scams going on at 1733 West Washburne. Mary Adams owned the property but "leased" it to Coleman. He in turn collected the rent, or as James Hickman put it, "beat the money out of people," for Adams. Coleman and Adams wanted the existing tenants out of the building so they could charge higher rents. Coleman then "leased" some of the building to Anthony Barnett, but the tenants still paid their rent to Coleman. All of this was an elaborate ruse to evade responsibility for providing legally required decent living conditions for the tenants. What exact role Anthony Barnett was playing in this wasn't clear. Was Coleman scamming him?

Willis, the Hickmans' eldest son and another survivor of that night, took the stand. He was still recovering from a broken collarbone that he received jumping from the third floor. Willis may not have felt like a hero when he took the stand, but his quick thinking and extraordinary strength that night had saved his mother and himself. The tornado of smoke and fire that consumed their room had prevented him from saving his young siblings.

"The smoke was all in the house," he told the jury, "and I did not see where we were, you cannot see good, and if I stayed in there one minute more, I would have been gone."

Ingles asked him where the children were when the fire flared up. Willis told him that there was so much smoke that he could not see where they were, and that he'd had to press a cloth or towel to his face to protect himself from the smoke.

Ingles, Nilson, and members of the jury didn't press him any further on this point. It was clear that he had done all that he could do. They moved on to a discussion of Coleman's threat. Willis never heard any threat directly from Coleman. In fact, Willis had never met him. "My father said that he [Coleman] said he had a man on the east side to burn that place down if he would only give the word."

Nilson then asked Willis about the center room, where he believed the fire began. Willis told the jury that just before the fire someone, he didn't know who, had removed a trunk and mattress from the center room. "The day the trunk was moved, the mattress was moved from the bed. It was not on there any more after that."

Nilson wanted to know if he had seen the can of kerosene in the center room. Willis said that he hadn't. Nilson pressed him on the point and asked him, "You are not there regularly?"

"No."

"I cannot remember seeing you," Nilson said.

"I work all the time."

Nilson was referring to the occasions when he inspected the building before the January 16 fire. Willis's testimony reinforced for Nilson that something was seriously wrong. "Somebody," Nilson declared, "had been in this room, taken those things out, but nobody seems to know who came up there, nobody claims this can either. I have talked to the people in the building."

Ingles closed the hearing and scheduled the next one for a week later, on February 13. Clearly frustrated about the way the state's attorney and the police were handling the Hickman case, he turned to Sergeant Madzinski. "State's Attorney Lang is going to subpoena those five or more people in here, from his office."

Madzinski meekly replied, "Yes."

Ingles pressed home the point: "I suggest that you talk to Mr. Lang. I will go out there with you."

Madzinski then asked if Ingles wanted Mrs. Adams subpoenaed.

"Have them all here" was his curt reply.

However, when Deputy Coroner Ingles called the third hearing into the deaths of the Hickman children into session on the morning of February 13, none of them were there. State's Attorney Lang, David Coleman, Mary Adams, and Anthony Barnett were absent.

Ingles called Madzinski to the stand to explain what had happened. He told Ingles that Lang had another trial that day. Annoyed, Ingles laid into Madzinski: "How about Coleman?"

"Coleman? I couldn't find him."

Irritated, Ingles asked: "Well, did you issue or serve him subpoenas?"

"No, sir. I didn't get no subpoenas to serve."

"Why is that?"

"I didn't get none from Lang," Madzinski answered lamely. "I was notified last night at four o'clock and told the hearing was going."

"At the last hearing," Ingles reminded him, "didn't we say we were going to subpoena those people?"

"Yes."

Madzinski went on to say that Coleman was due in court the following day on fraud charges. This didn't answer Ingles's question. He then tried to explain that he had tried to call Mary Adams but she didn't answer the phone. "I even tried to call this morning," Madzinski said, trying to salvage the situation. But of course, serving a subpoena in a case involving the horrific death of four children requires more effort than making a phone call. What was going on? Ingles directed Madzinski to serve Coleman a subpoena in court.

"Will you make it your business to see to it?"

Realizing that he couldn't rely on Madzinski alone to get these witnesses to the next coroner's hearing, Ingles turned to an unnamed police officer in the room. "I am going to give you the subpoenas, and you take care of it; give them to the Captain."

To make sure his orders were obeyed, he told the police officers, "I will call [Captain Lee Enright] and talk to him myself, and I am going to set this case over, then, and give you an opportunity to get this case in condition. We can't do anything without them."

A frustrated Ingles closed the hearing, declaring, "If this fire happened over on Sheridan Road [a wealthy strip of mansions on the north shore of Lake Michigan] someplace, we would have half the police force here."

"The kitchenette is our prison, our death sentence without trial."

6

"We the jury wish to go on record as condemning vigorously"

Mike Myer loved being a lawyer. "I'll quit when work stops being fun," he once told his brother-in-law Carl Shier. It never stopped being fun. And he was good at it. Ed Weinstein, a former law partner of Myer's, said with absolute conviction, "I'd stack him up against any lawyer in Chicago."

Myer worked in the historic Chicago Temple building in the city's busy Loop. The Temple, a tall sandstone office building, had long been home to many of the city's most prominent attorneys. The famed Clarence Darrow had an office on the sixth floor.

When the phone rang the morning following the Hickman fire, Myer had just arrived at work. Mike Bartell filled him in on the day's events, and Myer immediately went to work. He had a serious demeanor accentuated by the rimless glasses he wore. In private, he liked making bad puns, "real groaners," according to his daughter Linda. Myer was forty-one years old and five feet six inches tall—on the shorter end of medium height—and was beginning to develop the "stocky" build that plagues middle-aged men.

Myer had spent the better part of the previous year working on tenant issues, learning the ins and outs of the law and the byzantine workings of the OPA. Over the next few days he would help organize meetings on behalf of the Hickmans and was retained as the family's lawyer, filing a forty-thousand-dollar negligence suit against Mary Adams. This was the first case of SWP-inspired tenant organizing in Chicago that involved the deaths of children, possibly from arson. This added an extra urgency to his work but also new challenges. Myer had spent the bulk of his career as a "party attorney," earning little money and less notoriety in legal circles, largely working in the shadow of his mentor, the better-known Albert Goldman. Yet there were few attorneys as well prepared to handle the Hickman case as Mike Myer.

Meyer James Myer, or Mike to his friends, had been born Meyer Lebovsky on July 15, 1905, in the Ukrainian city of Katerynoslav. The city was named in honor of the eighteenth-century Russian empress Catherine the Great, when the Ukraine was part of the Russian empire. The Russia of his parents' generation was an extremely autocratic, repressive society. It was also an intensively anti-Semitic country. Jews had no civil rights under the czars and were the frequent victims of pogroms—violent mob rampages condoned by the authorities in an attempt to deflect growing popular opposition to the government and the aristocracy that stood behind it.

Myer's parents, Isaac and Rose Lebovsky, were Jews, and his mother's side of the family had a long association with radical underground politics. "My mother spoke of pogroms in 1895 and 1903. Her family had good relations with their Gentile neighbors, and her family was taken and protected by them." The effect of the state-sponsored bigotry expressed in pogroms was to make large numbers of Jews sympathetic to the socialist movement and eager to avail themselves of any opportunity to emigrate from the country.

After being drafted at the beginning of the Russo-Japanese War in 1904, Myer's father escaped from a Russian military assembly camp by bribing a guard. Isaac made his way back to Katerynoslav, quickly assembled his family, including his young daughter and infant son, and "left on a long, hazardous journey to America."

"As my father told it so many times, the trip was almost an unbelievable, harrowing adventure story," Mike recalled. Early on his mother was captured by border guards, but the family was later able to sneak out of an army camp and make another crossing, this one successful. They finally arrived in London in November and stayed for six weeks, and then traveled to Canada and then the United States. In a little more than three months, they had made their way from the southern Ukraine to Chicago.

Chicago was the transportation hub of the United States, with a vast network of railways that brought workers and raw materials in and sent out millions of tons of meat, manufactured goods, and steel girders for construction of the skyscrapers that became the hallmark of US cities. Chicago was also the capital of American radicalism, having been, in the 1880s, the center of the struggle for the eight-hour day. The city will be forever remembered in the international labor movement as the site of the infamous bombing of a workers' rally in Haymarket Square in 1886 and the subsequent framing and execution of the movement's leaders. It was also the site of the Pullman Strike of 1894, led by the soon-to-be Socialist Party (SP) orator and presidential candidate Eugene Debs. In the twentieth century, Chicago became the national headquarters of the SP, which would eventually grow to more than 100,000 members. The radical trade union Industrial Workers of the World (IWW), popularly known as "the Wobblies," led by "Big Bill" Haywood, held its first national convention in Chicago in 1905. The organizations that were later to merge to form the Communist Party were founded in Chicago in 1919, after a raucous convention split the Socialist Party.

The city had an equally notorious seamy side: open political corruption, ethnic rivalries, racist violence, bootlegging, and gang warfare. Al Capone became the very symbol of Chicago to the world in the 1920s. This was the city to which Mike Myer arrived as a baby in his mother's arms. It was a heady place to grow up.

Sometime after arriving in the United States, the Lebovsky family changed their surname to Myer. The name change was a convenient way for the family to distance itself from Isaac's draft and passport problems. Isaac was a skilled leatherworker and quickly found work in his trade in a suitcase factory, earning five dollars for a sixty-hour week. After a few years, he scraped together enough money to start his own business.

The radical sympathies of the Myer family were most evident in the parents' reading of the *Forward*, the daily socialist newspaper published in New York. Mike also read it as a teenager. He started college very young, at about sixteen, in 1921. He went to the University of Chicago for undergraduate studies and then on to its prestigious law school. After law school, Myer apprenticed as an attorney from October 1927 to April 1929 at the firm of Kixmiller & Barr in Chicago.

During this time he applied for US citizenship which he was granted on January 27, 1928, in Chicago. But the Myer family's tenuous hold on a lower-middle-class existence, like that of millions of other people, came to an end with the beginning of the Great Depression in 1929. Mike stepped up and helped with the family finances.

He also joined the SP in the early 1930s. Though the party was now only a shadow of its former self, it was growing under the impact of the economic crisis and the rise of fascism. A new radical left wing was also growing inside the SP, especially in its youth group, the Young People's Socialist League, better known by its acronym, YPSL (pronounced *yip-sil*).

Mike Myer's future wife, Belle Landau, attended Tuley High School in the early 1930s, when it had a reputation as "the Trotskyist high school" in Chicago. YPSL was the biggest grouping of radical Tuley students, with a basement headquarters near the campus, on California Street in the city's Humboldt Park neighborhood. Two teenage Trotskyists, Yetta Barshevsky and Natie Gould, were chosen to give the commencement speeches for the class of 1932, and electrified the audience when they tossed aside their faculty-approved speeches and gave a fiery attack on the capitalist system replete with quotes from Big Bill Haywood and Eugene Debs. Belle graduated from Tuley High the next year, 1933.

The American Trotskyists opted to join the SP in 1936 in an effort to increase their size and influence. They formed the appeal caucus in the SP and published two newspapers, one based in New York called *Socialist Appeal*, edited by Max Shachtman, and *Labor Action*, edited by James P. Cannon in San Francisco. A brilliant Chicago attorney, Albert Goldman, won Myer to Trotskyism. Goldman had been born Albert Verblen in Russia in 1897. He was seven years older than Myer and became a mentor to him in politics and the legal defense of radicals, trade unionists, and other victims of the criminal justice system.

Few other attorneys could claim the client list that Goldman could over his two-decade career. He defended unemployed workers as well as the most famous political refugee of the era, Leon Trotsky. Goldman was medium height with a shock of black hair. He shined in public with a sharp-edged intellect combined with practical courtroom experience.

One of his shining moments was his defense in 1941 of twenty-three men and women, including the national leaders of the SWP and leaders and members of the Minneapolis Teamsters Local 544. Goldman was among those indicted for violation of the 1861 Sedition Act (originally designed for use against the confederacy) and the Smith Act, which made it a felony to "teach, advocate, or encourage the overthrow or destruction of any such government by force or violence."

It's a rare situation when someone under the same indictment as his clients is their lead counsel. On October 27, 1941, Goldman put on a vigorous defense, challenging every aspect of the government's case, mocking its pretensions and skewering its witnesses. As his cocounsel, Mike Myer did much of the background legal work for the case. Goldman put James P. Cannon, SWP chairman, on the stand. Cannon gave clear and accessible answers about the party's political positions on a variety of issues. It was a tutorial on Marxism for the jury. Outside the courtroom, the SWP organized a nationwide defense campaign.

Five of the accused were acquitted on both counts of the indictment, and the remaining eighteen were found guilty only on the second count (violation of the Smith Act) and ordered to serve twelve to sixteen months in prison. The convicted defendants began to serve their sentences on December 31, 1943. The last prisoners were released in February 1945. Goldman in many ways suffered the severest consequences of the trial: the Illinois Bar Association disbarred him in 1943.

Mike Myer was not under indictment and became the SWP's lead attorney. He tried to appeal Goldman's disbarment, but despite his best efforts, he ultimately failed. He earned a modest income as a labor law attorney in Chicago, representing individual clients and local unions. He didn't know it yet, but with the Hickman case he was about to step out from under Goldman's shadow.

Five weeks had passed when Cook County coroner A. L. Brodie called to order the fourth and final hearing into the deaths of the Hickman children on February 27. The three previous hearings had put on public record the frightening conditions in which the Hickmans and other tenants lived and the callous response of Mary Adams to their pleas. The bloodcurdling threat of David Coleman to burn the building—a building full of children—had been exposed. The hearings explored Annie and Willis's terrifying escape the night of the fire, an escape that confounded and mystified veteran firefighter Chief Harry Nilson. The coroner's hearings had taken out of the shadows the private fears, struggles, and pain of the Hickman family. They had produced damning testimony against Adams and Coleman, both of whom had conspicuously avoided the hearings. There was strong circumstantial evidence that arson was the cause of the fire that had destroyed the attic and killed the Hickman children. How would Adams and Coleman respond to all of this?

This hearing was going to be very different from the previous ones; almost all the major players were present, with the notable exception of representatives from the State's Attorney's Office. Irving Lang, the assistant state's attorney who just a few weeks earlier had tried Coleman in felony court on larceny charges and argued that the judge should keep him in custody until the completion of the investigation into the fire, was absent. In the weeks that followed the rash of deadly tenement fires, Lang had been appointed by the State's Attorney's Office to lead the investigations into all these fires and recommend possible charges.

When Brodie called the hearing to order on February 27 at the Cook County morgue, he fully expected Lang or a representative of his office to be present. "Anyone representing the State's Attorney of Cook County?" Brodie turned to Sergeant Madzinski: "Did you hear from Assistant State's Attorney Lang?" Madzinski said that he had called Lang and told him when the hearing was but hadn't seen him. Brodie declared a one-hour recess to see "if he is on the way out here." When it became clear that no one from the State's Attorney's Office was coming, Brodie called the hearing back into session.

The first witness called to the stand was Mary Porter Adams, the person that most of the residents of 1733 West Washburne considered to be their real landlord. An attorney, David Wald, accompanied her. Her long-awaited appearance before the coroner's jury would address two major issues in the case: her relationship with David Coleman and the life-threatening conditions in her building. Adams told the jury that she had bought the building in 1945 and had sold it to David Coleman "on lease" in October 1946 for eight thousand dollars, with a down payment of three hundred. Coleman would pay her monthly installments until the full amount was paid off. Soon after the lease was signed, however, Adams and Coleman's business relationship soured. Coleman hadn't made any monthly payments since signing the lease, but she hadn't forfeited his contract.

Brodie found this whole relationship confusing and asked her, "Who has been receiving the rent from the property?"

She quickly responded, "Mr. Coleman received all the rents from the property."

Unfortunately, no one asked her about how she had come to meet Coleman. Was it as mundane as his answering her ad? Or did she or her husband have a prior relationship with him? What was her motivation for leasing the building? Had she ever checked into Coleman's past? The answers to these questions could have fleshed out more of the events that led to the fire.

Brodie moved the questioning toward Adams's care of the property and her relationship with her tenants. "During the time you owned the property, had you ever made any effort to modernize the apartments?"

Adams's haughty reply had the air of someone responding to an insult. "I certainly did. I have proof that I have spent some thirty three hundred dollars," she claimed, putting in new bathrooms with showers and "modernizing the plumbing." Her answer was at odds with the testimony by the tenants of her building and the findings of Chief Nilson from his inspections of the building.

Adams preferred to avoid this line of questioning by shifting the discussion back to her dealings with Coleman. She discovered that Coleman had subleased part of the building to a Mr. Anthony Lee Barnett. Coleman was racking up quite a track record of scamming money out of people. She tried to paint herself as a victim of thieving, ungrateful tenants and a corrupt business partner.

But then she made an admission that she perhaps thought was a clever move in her defense. Shortly after the New Year in 1947, she testified, Coleman's attorney contacted her attorney to say that his client was going to make amends and catch up on his delinquent payments. "We cannot let Mr. Coleman continue to collect rents, and not make payments," Adams's attorney allegedly told her. It would take at least a month to get the court to legally declare Coleman's lease forfeit, so she had herself appointed as an "agent" of the mortgage company that held her loan to collect the rents from her tenants, bypassing Coleman. For some reason, Adams thought that her being an "agent" absolved her of any responsibility for providing decent housing for her tenants.

Brodie jumped on this point. "Mrs. Adams, it seems from your interest, and collecting money, and you being a social worker, did you ever make any effort to alleviate such a situation as existed there? Did you ever make any effort to find any sanitary facilities for people living like they did in the attic, and the way people were living in the basement?"

"I most certainly did," she insisted. "I did everything I possibly could do at one time."

"Well," Brodie admonished her, "maybe that wasn't sufficient."

Adams defended herself. "I made all attempts to try to make a home for these people, of a suitable nature, and I never tried to evict any of the tenants. I never tried to cut the place up."

Of course, one of the first things Coleman had tried to do after he leased the building was "cut the place up." He couldn't have been doing this without her knowledge. The previous three hearings had documented extensively the inhumane conditions at 1733 West Washburne, including broken water pipes and a partially flooded basement. Thus Adams failed to make a dent in her image as an uncaring, greedy slumlord; if anything, she very successfully tied herself up in knots on the stand with her convoluted logic and feigned concern for her tenants.

At this point, the Hickman family's attorney, Myer, got a chance to cross-examine her. Myer thought there were still too many gaps in Adams's testimony concerning her relationship with Coleman. He zeroed in on these. "You say you sold this property to Mr. Coleman sometime in October?"

"That's right."

"Was that by deed or contract?"

"On contract."

"Contract?"

"Yes."

"And was that contract recorded?"

"I don't know if Mr. Coleman recorded it or not."

"Did *you* record the contract?"

"No, I didn't."

This short, simple exchange clearly established that Adams held the deed to the property and that for all intents and purposes Coleman was working for her.

Myer then moved on to her relationship with her tenants. "All right, now, you say you never tried to evict any tenants?" Adams emphatically denied it.

Myer picked up an eviction notice to show her but he was interrupted by Brodie.

"Are you trying to establish personal liability here, basis for a civil suit, or what?" Brodie and other city and county officials were unhappy with Myer's presence, despite Brodie's sympathy for the Hickmans. This was the officials' turf and they didn't like being upstaged.

"I am trying to establish the fact," explained Myer, "that she was responsible, one of the people responsible for the conditions there, and that she is guilty none-the-less for criminal negligence."

"We are interested in finding out," said Brodie, "who was responsible for the conditions resulting in the death of these four children."

"Yes, so am I, and I am trying to show that she was in active management during this period."

Myer had a point, and Brodie allowed him to continue. Myer turned to Adams and, pointing to the signature at the bottom of the notice, asked, "Is this your signature at the bottom of this paper, which purports to be a Landlord's Five Day Notice?"

She replied that it was. The notice was dated January 11, 1947, six days before the fire. It was addressed to Will Johnson, another 1733 West Washburne tenant.

Brodie interrupted again. He wanted to see this notice for himself. He may have been annoyed by the presence of a radical attorney in his hearing, but when that attorney had material evidence that should have been given to him by police investigators, that may have made him angry. It may have made him even angrier that a key witness had so boldfacedly contradicted her testimony in front of him.

Mary Adams then offered this explanation:

I gave Mr. Johnson that, because Mr. Johnson called me up the other day and we went out there Sunday before [the fire], and he told me that he was going to call in the plumber and have the water fixed there, and fixed in his own apartment, and pay it out of rents . . . I tried to reason with him in a logical manner, in a logical manner, and he said: "I don't care what you say, I am going to hire a plumber, have him come in here, and fix all this old plumbing." I said, Mr. Johnson, if you do that, I will have to have you leave, I cannot have that in your apartment, you will have to give it up. Now, that explains that.

If Mary Adams thought that this was going shift the blame for the living conditions at 1733 West Washburne from her to Coleman, she was mistaken.

Myer pressed Brodie and Earl Downes (representing the fire department) for their position on this point for the record. Downes tried to evade answering by attacking Myer for conducting a "fishing expedition" but then reluctantly conceded, "She was running the building."

"I think that it has been established from the evidence this morning," Brodie conceded, "that Mrs. Adams had been running the building, [and] had been collecting rents—that has been brought out."

"That satisfies me," said Myer. "That's the first thing I wanted cleared up—as long as we are clear on this."

Yet in the days leading up to the fire, Coleman was still legally the lessee of the building. Though he and Adams may have been at loggerheads, that didn't mean that he was willingly forfeiting their contract, and she hadn't forfeited it either. Nothing in Coleman's history with the tenants suggested that he was tired of getting his hands on their money or wouldn't fight Adams for control of the property. Adams may have leased the building to him to have him deal with her combative tenants, but she ended up in a business relationship with a man as unscrupulous as she was and, by many accounts, willing to use threats of violence to get his way.

David Coleman sat in the hearing room with everyone else listening to Adams's bizarre testimony. It must have been very difficult, at the very least, for the tenants of 1733 West Washburne to be sitting so close to a man who had brought such fear into their lives. As for the surviving members of the Hickman family, we can only guess at the pain and anger they must have felt when they looked at the man.

Coleman's strategy on the stand was similar to that of Adams—deny any wrongdoing and try to paint the tenants as irrational. He explained that he lived at 2720 South Prairie, the north end of the South Side ghetto in Chicago, and he worked as a mechanic. Calling himself the "contract owner" of 1733 West Washburne, he said that he had taken possession of the building in late July 1946.

After these preliminary questions were answered, Downes and Brodie vigorously interrogated him. Downes asked Coleman whether he had taken money from James Hickman on the promise of a better apartment. He denied it. Brodie asked him to explain the shabby, dangerous condition of the building. "Under that lease, were you required to do any repairs, and operate the building properly, with respect to proper repairs and other facilities, as required by city ordinances?"

Coleman said he was. "I had men over there to do the work, they could not get in, tenants put them out when they go to work."

The tenants had thrown the contractors out of the building because they had come to cut their apartments into smaller ones, not because they were there to fix broken pipes, exposed wires, or other structural problems with the building. Downes went after him on this.

"During the time from November seventh, you tried to repair this building, by 'building' you intended to build it up into separate apartments, that is, into separate apartments?"

Coleman tried to evade giving a straight answer, calling it "repair work."

Downes then asked him whether he ever had any trouble with the tenants at 1733 West Washburne.

Coleman again tried to evade giving a straight answer, then reluctantly conceded, "Yes."

Downes kept pressing Coleman on this point, and he painted himself into a corner.

"Did you have trouble with four or five of the tenants, Mr. Coleman, over the reconstruction program there?"

"Well, they had trouble with the contractor."

"I ask you, if you had any personal trouble with these people there, about the construction work you'd contemplated?"

"No, I didn't."

"You did not?"

"No."

"Is it not a fact," Downes pressed, "in talking to them you said they would move out, or, either you would stick a match to it, or burn them out, anything like that?"

"No."

"Did you say that?"

"No, I didn't."

"And nobody here heard you say that, nobody here ever heard you say that, because you never said anything like that, is that correct?"

"Yes."

Brodie posed the question point-blank to Coleman. "Mr. Coleman, have you ever told any one of the tenants, or the neighbors, in substance, you would burn the building down?"

"No sir, never said that to nobody."

Downes and Brodie had set the stage for Coleman to get a pummeling. They called to the stand one tenant after another to repeat Coleman's threat to them.

James Hickman reported that Coleman had told him, "Hickman, I've got men on the east side who'll stick fire to this building if I told them to."

Julia Rogers testified that Coleman told her, "I will get you out of there if it takes a fire."

Will Jackson recalled Coleman saying, "I will get everybody out of here when I want to if it takes fire. I have a man on the south side that will do just like I ask."

This was devastating testimony against David Coleman. Yet virtually everyone in the room understood that the issues involved in the death of the Hickman children were not just about one building or one landlord.

The Black communities of Chicago were plagued by housing conditions like those the Hickmans and other tenants of 1733 West Washburne were forced to endure and were devastated by fires that particularly victimized children and the elderly.

For people like A. L. Brodie, the Great Chicago Fire of 1871 always loomed in the background. In the middle of the final hearing, Brodie tried to put the Hickman tragedy in context for the jury: "Types of fires like this started the largest conflagration, the largest fire in the history of the country, the great Chicago conflagration. We have a good Fire department in Chicago, it is adequate in every respect, but if we have a dozen or so fires, breaking out at one time in the City of Chicago, we wouldn't have enough men or equipment to do much about it. I say all that to show how important it is to keep property in such condition so it will not be a hazard to life, limb, and property itself."

Brodie then turned to the jury to instruct them on how to deliberate on their verdict regarding the cause of the deaths of the Hickman children. The jury was made up of six men. Their last names were Haugh, Costello, Martin, Nolan, Balcher, and Kamp. Given the preponderance of Irish and German names and the thick fog of racism that enveloped the city, it is almost a certainty that all of them were white. Brodie reported to them that the coroner's physician, Dr. J. J. Kearns, had examined all the bodies of the four Hickman children and determined that the cause of death was extensive second-degree burns and shock.

He then went on to summarize the keys issues for the jury to consider.

We have considerable testimony with respect to a statement showing there is arson involved here . . . I am going to ask the jury, when their findings are ready, that they make recommendations that this matter be further investigated by the State's Attorney's Office of Cook County . . . I mean, that it was possible, that during the course of the fire, considering as a factor that a man was seen running down the stairs, a kerosene can was found up there, and here we have witnesses to testify that there has been threats made by this man about burning the building down unless everybody moved out, that makes the testimony inconclusive. At any rate, I will now ask the jury to retire and deliberate on a proper verdict.

At this point Mike Myer asked the coroner to request that the jury consider another issue in their deliberations, "that there be further investigation" into "who was responsible for permitting people to live under those conditions."

"Evidently," he added, "most of the ordinances of the city were violated, and I think the Coroner should take notice of that in his findings."

Brodie replied that he would leave that up to the discretion of the jurors.

The jurors retired to a separate room and began their deliberations. Shortly thereafter J. Haugh, the jury foreman, announced that they had reached a verdict, and the jurors returned to the hearing room. Brodie asked all of them if they had reached a verdict, and they replied at once, "We have." Haugh handed the written verdict to Brodie, who read it into the record. After summarizing the facts of the case, he then moved to the substance of the verdict.

We the jury wish to go on record as condemning vigorously, the condition existing at premises herein, both as to sanitation, as well as a place for human habitation. We wish to call to the attention of the proper authorities of the City of Chicago, and County of Cook, the conditions as set forth, which existed in violation of all Codes laws, and/or Ordinances governing places for human abode, and especially do we wish to condemn the practice of the landlord, owner or agent of said premises for permitting such conditions to exist, and for such profit-making theory as exercised therein, as we the jury feel such premises, as set forth herein, should be condemned by the City of Chicago, and wrecked, to avoid future reoccurrences.

From the testimony presented, we the jury are UNABLE TO DETERMINE whether said occurrence as ACCIDENTAL, or of an INCENDIARY nature, therefore, we the jury recommend that this case, together with the record, be turned over to the State's Attorney of Cook County, for further investigation, with emphasis placed on housing conditions, particularly in segregated areas, affecting human lives.

Brodie asked the jurors whether this was their unanimous verdict, and they all said, "Yes, sir." He closed the inquest and said to the jurors, "Thank you gentlemen, very kindly—that is a very fine verdict." He declared the hearing at an end. David Coleman and Mary Adams got up from their seats and walked past the surviving members of the Hickman family and out the door.

"When I got to summing up my life I saw my life was unhappy. I was in grief and sorrow."

7
"God is my secret judge"

"I'm putting the law down," declared Irving Lang. "If a tenant loses his life on property during a fire as a result of violation of the building code, the owner would face a murder charge."

As the spring of 1947 approached, fires continued to burn their way though the city's Black neighborhoods. "Negroes Half of City's Fire Toll as 5 More Die" was the front-page story of the *Chicago Defender* for March 15, 1947. Lang, like many others, was outraged. He was one of the liberals in the Cook County State's Attorney's Office, a place notorious for turning a blind eye to corruption in city and county politics and the needs of Chicago's Black community.

Born in 1912, Lang had grown up on Chicago's Jewish West Side. His parents were immigrants from the Ukraine. and his mother owned a millinery shop right next door to the Madison Theater. Lang had studied to be an aeronautical engineer at the University of Michigan, but the Depression led him to switch to what he hoped would be a more practical profession—the law. He transferred to the University of Chicago, where he earned an undergraduate degree in political science and a law degree, graduating in 1937 just in time for the "Roosevelt Recession." After a frustrating attempt to establish his own law practice, he was hired on at the Cook County State's Attorney's Office, where he worked as an assistant state's attorney handling major felony cases for the next two decades (minus his war years as a lieutenant in the navy).

Lang's threat to prosecute landlords for murder was sparked by the fire deaths of two children, Ronald and Gerald Phillips. The Phillips family—William and Susan and their sons, four-year-old Ronald and two-year-old Gerald—had lived in a rear one-room apartment on the second floor of 2001 West Fulton on Chicago's West Side. The room was unheated and barely accommodated the two beds that the Phillipses slept in. There were a total of five families in seven rooms on the second floor, and all the building's residents were African American. A storefront church occupied most of the first floor.

Wash Lamkin, Ronald and Gerald's grandfather, lived across the hall from the Phillipses. Lamkin's room was one of the few in the building with heat. He had a coal stove and would let Susan and her children stay in his room during the cold winter days. William Phillips was a truck driver and mostly worked at night.

The Phillipses had been living in the apartment for nearly six months when tragedy struck. On the night of March 6, 1947, around 9:00 p.m., Susan wanted to get the boys to bed. Gerald was at his grandfather's, while Ronald was in the family's room. Suddenly Susan saw a flame and smoke shoot out of the Phillipses' room. "Smoke!" she heard her son Ronald scream. She called to Ronald to get out, but he shouted back that he couldn't. Susan ran down the hall and asked a woman in the front apartment to call the fire department. Ronald dashed through the smoke and flames into his grandfather's room and got under the bed with his younger brother. By this time the fire was spreading down the hall. Susan helped Wash Lamkin out of the building and pulled the alarm at fire box 532. The door slammed closed behind her, and she was locked out. It was 9:15 p.m. The Phillips boys were trapped.

Firefighter Maurice McCarthy was driving his chief back to the fire station when he received a radio call about a house fire. He immediately swung around and headed for 2001 West Fulton. By then other firefighters had tried to get into the building to rescue the Phillips boys, but the smoke and flames were too overwhelming. They were now focused on hosing down the building. McCarthy's car screeched to a halt at the corner of Damen and Fulton, and a frenzied Susan Phillips told them that her children were trapped upstairs. The chief turned to McCarthy: "Go and see if you can get them out." By this time fire had engulfed the entire second floor, but McCarthy and several other firefighters kicked down the front door and went up the stairs.

On the second floor, McCarthy found himself inside an inferno. Fire was pouring out of two or three of the rooms. He wasn't sure which room the Phillips boys were in, so they searched them all.

"I found the one and I handed that one to another fellow, he took that one out and continued to search and found the other little lad [Gerald] right under the head of the bed up against the wall." They called for an ambulance and it took them to County Hospital. Ronald and Gerald had suffered second-degree burns and smoke inhalation. Ronald was the first to die, declared dead at 12:30 p.m. Gerald hung on until the next morning.

Lulu Dare, an elderly resident living on a pension, barely escaped with her life. She lived in the front of the building and was helped out of her second-floor window by a neighbor. The fire gutted the entire second floor.

William Phillips came home to his distraught but physically unharmed wife. He was given the painful task of identifying the bodies of his sons at the county morgue. They had lost everything in the fire. "We don't save nothing. We hardly have clothes to put on—the neighbors had to help us out," William later lamented at the coroner's hearing. When Deputy Coroner Ingles asked William Phillips and Lulu Dare what might have caused the fire, neither could give a definite answer, but both pointed to defective wiring in the room. (Dare had lived in the Phillipses' room before she moved to the front of the building.) A short in the socket of the overhead light caused long periods when the lights were simply not working.

"It has been that way for three years, you say?" asked Ingles.

"Yes, sir," Dare answered. "Three years in February, I have been there. I used to live in the same room, long before these people [the Phillipses]."

William Phillips told the coroner's jury that he would have fixed the defective wiring himself. The landlord was aware of the problem and sent a handyman to fix it, but the defective wiring was never replaced. No definitive cause of the fire that killed the Phillips boys was ever established, but Ingles believed from the testimony that the defective wiring was the cause. It is likely that Ronald Phillips had pulled the chain to turn on the overhead light and the loose wiring sparked a fire. The coroner's jury ruled the deaths of Ronald and Gerald Phillips an accident. While no one had set this fire, the coroner's hearing again highlighted dangerous living conditions for Chicago's African Americans.

The coroner's jury had recommended that the case of the death of the Hickman children "be turned over to the State's Attorney of Cook County, for further investigation, with emphasis placed on housing conditions, particularly in segregated areas, affecting human lives." Yet despite the powerful testimony at the coroner's hearings and the jury's strongly worded recommendation, the state's attorney and the Chicago police did not pursue a murder investigation.

No one from the Chicago Police Department or the State's Attorney's Office ever formally interviewed any member of the Hickman family. The powerful banks and real estate and insurance companies whose towering edifices dominated the Loop skyline had a thousand tentacles that reached into every aspect of political power in the city and twisted them in their interests. James Hickman was known only to a handful of the people who directed the life of the city, and some had already fixed the system so delinquent landlords would only be slapped with petty fines despite the mounting fire death toll. David Coleman and Mary Adams, who would not have been allowed to use the front door of the homes of these powerful white businessmen and political leaders, were protected even if they weren't fully aware of it. Irving Lang may have wanted to charge landlords who deliberately neglected their property with murder, but at the end of the day they were simply given measly fines. Coleman was eventually fined a total of $350 plus $250 for fire and building code violations and the failure to get a permit for construction, the equivalent of $150 for each of the lives of the Hickman children.

After the fire, Willis Hickman was able to secure housing built for returning veterans for the surviving members of his family—the first floor of 7805 South Kolin, a small house with a front porch in the Ashburn Park neighborhood of Chicago. By now it had been two months since the younger Hickman children had died. Willis, Charles, and Annie watched their beloved father and husband sink deeper into depression. Many weekday evenings Willis would come home from working long hours at the post office and find his father sitting alone in the living room. Though the lights were on, he seemed to be sitting in the dark. He would sit for long periods with his eyes closed, saying nothing. His breathing was slow and deliberate, and he seemed to be lost somewhere deep inside himself.

"Before the fire he was outgoing," Willis later reported. "Not after the fire."

Willis was unsure of how to respond to his father's intense loneliness. "He wouldn't eat. He had nothing say." Sometimes his eyes would open and the two of them would do small chores together. Mostly, though, James just looked around the empty house. His oldest sons had moved out, and his younger children were dead. He tried to comfort himself with memories of the little ones, but it only brought more pain. The young ones used to bring a glass of water to their thirsty father when he came home from work. They would crowd around him and ask, "Daddy, have you any candy?"

Coleman's threats kept going through James's head "like a clock, over and over again." The images of his deceased children filled his mind. "Paper was made to burn, coal and rags," James told his son Willis. "Not people. People wasn't made to burn."

It was one day in March that James Hickman walked into Mages Sport Store at the corner of Sixty-Third Street and South Halstead to buy a gun. Mages advertised itself as one of "Chicago's Leading Dealers in Sporting Goods for Every Sport" ("Whatever the Sport—We Have the Equipment"), goods that included revolvers, pistols, shotguns, and rifles. James scanned display cases filled with various makes, models, and calibers of handguns. One caught his eye. It was a Mauser .32-caliber blue steel automatic pistol with a white handle in a black leather holster. James held it in his hand and tried on the holster.

The Mages salesman refused to sell it to him over the counter, however, probably because James didn't have a permit from the police department. The salesman told him that the way around this was to have the gun mailed to him—like buying it via mail-order catalog. So James Hickman paid $37.50 for the pistol, the holster, and a small box of ammunition and had them mailed to his daughter Arlena's apartment on the South Side. A few days later, he picked up the package, brought it home, and locked the gun in the family "money box" underneath his and Annie's bed. The gun was for their protection, he told Annie. James still hadn't decided whether he was going to kill David Coleman.

Meanwhile, the fire epidemic continued.

Albert Hill was sixty-three years old and had very limited mobility. His right leg had been amputated years earlier, and he was missing most of his left foot. Living alone on the second floor of a two-story building at 323 North Clarement on Chicago's West Side, he was dependent on his neighbors for meeting his daily needs. The building had been cut up into seven one-room apartments, all inhabited by African Americans.

The fire began around midnight on the first floor and spread quickly to the second. Thelma Cribbs, a neighbor of Hill's, heard shouting and woke her husband, Rozzie. "I ran out and opened the door and I saw the blaze was coming to my door, and I went to get my husband out of the door. That is when he got his hair singed," she later told the coroner's jury.

Fred Johnson and his wife lived next to Albert Hill. "My wife jumped up from bed and said, 'Oh, the house is on fire.'" Johnson reached for his clothes and told his wife, "Get the rest of the children out." He heard Hill shouting from the room next door, "Don't leave me!" Johnson opened the door to Hill's room but was pushed back by flames and deadly smoke that nearly burned his face. "Well, all I had to do is put my hand and feel around for him and that fire and smoke was so bad I missed him. I couldn't get him."

Sixteen of the residents who were home at the time of the fire gathered outside in the clear, cold early spring night. The fast-moving fire had unnerved of all them, so much that only a few had tried to wake their neighbors before they fled in fear for their lives.

Fred Johnson's wife had been awakened by shouts from his aunt, who lived across the street. "My auntie said the fire had been plentiful along, and it wakened her up. The rest of the people were downstairs, I told them I reckon they should get us woke up. Nobody was to wake us up but my auntie."

When firefighters arrived, flames were shooting out of the windows and the roof.

"We were told there was a person in there," recalled Fred Becker, a firefighter with the Eighteenth Battalion. "We worked our way up in the rear stairway, and on our hands and knees, groped around to find him, and we found him in a small bedroom. He was lying in front of the cot. And he was dead at that time. We removed him."

The fire spread so fast that Deputy Coroner Ingles initially suspected arson. "That is the strange part of it, how these flames traveled so far without anybody finding out about it, and traveled up to the second floor before anybody knew anything about it." But the origins of the fire were traced back to a portable heater on the first floor that had apparently overheated and burned into the floor, starting the inferno. Police officer Thomas Tuitt, who investigated Albert Hill's death, considered it "a wonder how they got out, the way the building was. [The fire] just enveloped the whole building at once." The outer walls were the only parts left standing—the interior of the building was totally gutted.

One day in April, Willis Hickman heard a strange sound from his parents' bedroom. He edged toward the bedroom door and turned his head to listen carefully. It was his father speaking softly to someone. Then he heard his father say "Velvina and Elzina," the names of his deceased sisters. Willis struggled to hear what his father was saying, but it was difficult to follow his words. Then James's voice grew louder and more agitated. Willis began to back away from the door. "The Lord have mercy," James cried out and ran out of the bedroom, right past him.

The deaths of his youngest children had been like a shadow that followed James everywhere. When he got home, he couldn't keep it in any longer. "He used to carry on practically every day," Annie recalled. He would sit down at the dinner table and start talking about his deceased children. "My children got no cause to be dead. Other children are playing. My children have a right to play too. They didn't do any harm." The more he talked, the more agitated he became. David Coleman's threat to burn him out was never far from his mind. "I know what Coleman told me. After he said it would happen, it did happen."

The six-month anniversary of the fire was rapidly approaching. On July 10, the Progressive Steelworkers Union (PSWU) called for a strike against Wisconsin Steel. Despite its left-wing-sounding name, it was essentially a company union, but it was under pressure from its membership to act. The union was demanding a closed shop and pay for six holidays. James didn't participate in strike activity; he stayed home alone. With his routine disrupted, he fell into a deeper depression.

On July 15, the day before the anniversary of the fire that took away his children, James got into an argument with Annie about going to church, but ended up going anyway. After the services there was a social event, and they didn't get home until nearly midnight. James didn't go to bed. He sat in the living room holding photos of his deceased children. His lips moved slowly as he gazed at them. Many years earlier in Mississippi he had made a solemn pledge to God to protect his family. He was going to keep that promise, but he wrestled with what to do. Exhausted, he finally went to bed.

James Hickman woke up on the morning of July 16 and at first felt calm. "I wasn't mad, I wasn't glad," he later told journalist John Bartlow Martin. The calm soon dissipated. He was uneasy, struggling with his inner feelings. Something was calling him. Annie watched him as he paced the living room, back and forth.

Then he suddenly darted into the bedroom and reached underneath the bed for the cash box containing the pistol. He brought the box into the living room, snapped the key off his belt, and opened it. He took the pistol out and pulled it from the holster. He had been around guns ever since he was young in Mississippi. But this one was different. It wasn't for shooting rattlesnakes or menacing animals.

James set the gun on the table in front of him and started pacing the room, his eyes never leaving the pistol. He didn't say a word to Annie, who sat silently watching him. He picked up the gun, looked at it, put it down again. Later he told Martin that right up until the moment he left his home he was strongly resisting the urge to confront David Coleman with a gun in his hand.

He kept saying over and over again, "I can't go through with this." But a voice inside him kept speaking, reminding him of his pledge to protect his children. He believed that it was the voice of God. James picked up the pistol for the third time, and this time he loaded it. He strapped on the holster and shoved the pistol in. He grabbed a light jacket and put it on. More pacing. Then he walked out, came back, left the house again, and again came back. The third time he left, he caught a streetcar.

July 16, 1947, was a Wednesday, a busy day in a busy city. The weather was mild, with temperatures in the low eighties. The humidity, however, rose by the hour, a sure sign that heavy rains and lightning were on their way. The streetcars were full of people. James must have been conscious of the weight of the gun hidden inside his jacket. The streetcar sped north. Did he bristle when men and women brushed past him on their way out the door? Did any of them feel the gun?

All morning he was struggling with his feelings. Distracted, uncomfortable, and restless, he was acting like a man being dragged to an appointment he didn't want to keep. When the streetcar neared Twenty-Sixth and Prairie Avenue, James pulled the stop cord, got off, and started walking. It was about one o'clock in the afternoon when he got to Coleman's block.

"I stood there on the street. *I didn't want to go through with what it was telling me* . . . [But] this was a vow that I made to this family."

The 2700 block of South Prairie Avenue was lined with mansions whose glory days were long past. It was here in the summer of 1946 that James Hickman had first met David Coleman.

The street was mostly empty, and the sight of a Black man walking down it was not out of the ordinary. From a distance James spotted Coleman. He was sitting in his half-brother Percy Brown's taxicab, a big four-door Buick sedan, on the west side of the street in front of his house. Coleman was holding court, reading a newspaper story out loud to two men next to the car. He had a big smile on his face and periodically let out a booming laugh. Two men were laughing with him. One of them, Percy, saw the man coming toward them. He later testified that it was James Hickman, but at that moment he didn't recognize him and thought nothing of it. He turned his attention back his brother, leaning through one of the side windows of the cab to listen to him. Charles McLaurin, a friend of Percy's, was installing "fog lights" on the front of the car.

Hickman didn't have to go to Coleman's front door and run the risk of encountering Coleman's wife and kids. Looking at the two men laughing with Coleman, he must have wondered whether either of them was the "man on the East Side" who Coleman had said was ready to set a fire. Coleman's attention was focused on his newspaper. Hickman startled him when he appeared, standing no more than three feet away. It seemed as if he had come out of nowhere. Hickman's friendly demeanor puzzled him even more.

"How do you do, how are you feeling this morning, Coleman?"

"What do you want with me?"

"I come to ask you something about this arrest warrant, of the $100 and causing this disturbance." Presumably, Hickman was referring to the fire.

"Yes, but I ain't going to pay you."

James Hickman finally went over the edge. "My mind got scattered," he later recalled, at the moment when he pulled out his pistol and started shooting.

Coleman was sitting in the driver's seat of the cab. The left side of Coleman's body was closest to Hickman. When Hickman pointed the gun at Coleman and fired, the barrel was extremely close to Coleman's body. The first two bullets entered the upper part of Coleman's left shoulder and neck and lodged there. They tore ragged wounds in Coleman's spinal cord, and blood gushed out all over his clothes and the seat of the car.

Percy Brown began to back away from the car. Charles McLaurin dropped his tools, stood up, and began to back away as well. Hickman turned his attention to Brown and told him not to move, but Brown started to run. James pointed his gun at him and fired two shots. He missed. Brown and McLaurin fled, dodging around parked cars to get away from the man with the gun.

Hickman turned back to Coleman, who was still alive and conscious. He later recalled having the following exchange with the mortally wounded man.

"I'll pay you," Coleman gasped.

"It's too late now. God is my secret judge. You started the fire."

"Yes, I did."

"I shot him twice more," Hickman later recounted. One of these shots missed Coleman, but a third bullet passed through his neck. Bleeding profusely, he passed out. Hickman thought he had killed him right then and there, but Coleman was still alive.

James Hickman walked south on Prairie Avenue and put the gun in the holster under his jacket. He caught a streetcar at Twenty-Ninth and Indiana Avenue that took him west to Thirty-First and Wentworth, where he caught another streetcar home. On his way home, a sense of relief washed over him. "I put a heavy load down and a big weight fell off of me and I felt light."

At 1:14 p.m., Sergeant Jason Driscoll, at the Third District police station, received a call that a man had been shot at 2720 South Prairie. Percy Brown ran into the station to report the shooting at about the same time. Detectives John A. Nevelle and Leo Connolly, along with officers Hogan, McFadden, McMullen, and Rinehart, were assigned to the case. Willie Howard, a neighbor of Coleman's and witness to the shooting, put the unconscious, heavily bleeding Coleman in his car and took him to Michael Reese Hospital.

By the time police arrived at the scene of the shooting, Coleman was already at the hospital. The doctors there stopped the bleeding but didn't operate to remove the bullets. Coleman soon regained consciousness. He was then transferred to Cermak Hospital, adjacent to the Cook County Jail at Twenty-Sixth and California. This hospital cared for prisoners who were ill, and the police also used it to house material witnesses and criminal suspects wounded during the course of a criminal act.

When James Hickman walked through the front door of his house, Charles was the only one home. He asked Charles where his mother was, and Charles said she was at Arlene's apartment. James told him to go get her, because he had something to tell her.

Annie was fully aware of the torment inside her husband and the struggle that he had gone through that morning. When she came into the house and saw him, she expected the worst. They sat down together at the table with Charles, and James told them everything.

"They will find you," Annie said.

"I know," James replied.

Annie noticed that the torment had left her husband. He seemed at ease for the first time since the family had come to Chicago. James put the gun back in the "money box" and gave the key to Annie. He told Charles to wait on the porch for the police, and he and Annie settled themselves on the couch in the living room.

It wasn't until around 6:30 p.m. that the Homicide Squad arrived at 7805 South Kolin. Sergeant Seymour Stein led the squad in a rush up the stairs onto the porch, where Charles was waiting. Stein asked Charles where his father was, and he pointed inside. The squad entered the small house and found Annie and James sitting in the living room waiting for them. Stein and his men surrounded James and handcuffed him. Stein barked questions at James as two of the uniformed police officers held his arms. "We questioned him and he admitted shooting David Coleman over one hundred dollars," he later told his superiors.

Stein asked Annie Hickman if she was aware that her husband had done this, and she said yes. He asked her where the gun was, and she quickly gave him the key to the money box and told him it was under the bed. Stein went into their bedroom and opened the box; inside it he found the pistol, eight cartridges, and the black leather holster. He came out, held up the gun, and asked James whether this was the gun with which he had shot Coleman. James said it was. Stein led James in handcuffs out of his home, and the men all got into car 19 and drove Hickman to the Detective Bureau.

After filling out some paperwork at the Detective Bureau, Stein turned Hickman over to patrolmen James Micus and Charles Martin, who took him to Cermak Hospital to be identified by Coleman. Micus and Martin brought Hickman in handcuffs to Coleman's room. Coleman could not speak because of the gunshot wounds to his neck, but he identified Hickman as the man who shot him by nodding his head slightly. Micus and Martin reported that Hickman "admitted it in front of [Coleman], that he shot him." Coleman was unable to sign a statement because the bullets had "severed a number of nerves and tendons causing a complete paralysis of both arms."

Immediately after being identified by Coleman, Hickman was taken to the Chicago Police Department's Third District headquarters around 9:00 p.m. for interrogation. He gave a signed confession to Micus and Martin. He showed no hesitation in confessing to shooting Coleman and his reasons for doing it.

When asked to explain "in your own way" what happened, Hickman said, "I said you got my hundred dollars and you started the building on fire and you caused a lot of unhappiness in my home. I shot him twice and then I stepped back and a man ran away from the car and I said to this man don't make a move. I had a gun in my left hand, and I went back to the car again, and Coleman said Hickman I'll pay you your hundred dollars and I said to him 'Coleman you set the building on fire didn't you?' and he said 'Yes' and I shot at him two more times."

In his report to the commander of the Third District, Detective Nevelle described Hickman's shooting of Coleman as part of an "old feud." After signing his statement confessing to the shooting of Coleman, Hickman was loaded into a patrol wagon with other prisoners and transported west across the city to the Cook County Jail on the city's Southwest Side. At this point he wasn't facing a murder charge. But that would soon change.

"...And I weakened down to the ground"

8

"Did shoot, kill and murder"

Mike Myer, like tens of thousands of other Chicagoans, learned about the shooting of David Coleman two days later, from the *Chicago Tribune*. "Landlord Shot, Seize Dad of 4 Killed by Fire," it reported on the morning of July 18. "The prisoner [James Hickman] admitted the shooting, saying his children are dead because Coleman failed to make agreed repairs on the building." The three-paragraph-long article on page 14 went on to say that David Coleman was in serious condition. Sergeant Seymour Stein, one of Hickman's arresting officers, appeared to be the *Tribune*'s source for the story. Coleman was now in critical condition at Cook County Hospital, where doctors still feared to operate on him to remove the two bullets lodged in his neck and shoulder.

Myer knew James Hickman as a deeply religious man who had never harmed anyone in his life. Myer had had very little contact with the Hickman family of late. He and his friend Leon Despres were still representing the tenants of 1733 West Washburne. The previous month, they had successfully stopped an effort by Mary Adams to evict the remaining tenants.

The *Chicago Defender* reported that her eviction suit was "thrown out of renters court, and saved six families, including 15 adults and 20 children from being put out of their fire damaged home."

Though Myer had represented the Hickman family at the fourth coroner's hearing and filed a civil wrongful death suit against Adams on their behalf, neither James nor anyone else from the Hickman family had tried to contact him following the shooting. Annie Hickman did speak to the pastor of her church, who recommended that she contact William Temple, a well-known Black criminal defense attorney who had once been famed boxer Joe Louis's lawyer. James Hickman had been held in custody for nearly two days without legal counsel and appeared to have confessed to trying to kill Coleman. The dramatic turn of events had overwhelmed the Hickman family.

When Myer reached his office, he called Mike Bartell and told him that he was going over to the County Jail. Meanwhile, Coleman's critical condition was beginning to deteriorate.

On the morning of July 17, 1947, James Hickman was brought to the County Jail, where he would spend the next six months of his life.

The Cook County courthouse and jail are imposing, ominous buildings that are difficult to access; they look strangely out of place in their largely working-class Southwest Side neighborhood adjoining a modest business district on Twenty-Sixth Street. Earlier courthouses and jails in Chicago had been in or near the Loop, near all the other institutions of city, county, state, and federal government. The Haymarket Martyrs had been tried in the courthouse built after the Great Fire of 1871 on Hubbard Street, just north of the Loop, and had been executed at the adjacent county jail on Clark Street. Clarence Darrow had pleaded some of his most famous cases in the same courthouse.

In 1902, Darrow accepted an invitation from the warden of Cook County Jail to address the inmates on the subject of crime and criminals. What the warden had expected from his renowned guest lecturer is anybody's guess, but the lanky, disheveled Darrow delivered a passionate attack on the criminal justice system in the jail's auditorium: "Courts are not instruments of justice. When your case gets into court it will make little difference whether you are guilty or innocent, but it's better if you have a smart lawyer. And you cannot have a smart lawyer unless you have money. First and last it's a question of money. Those men who own the earth make the laws to protect what they have."

Undoubtedly many in the audience agreed, but one inmate complained that the lecture was "too radical." Some of Darrow's more genteel friends and supporters were aghast at his audacity. "Your theories might be true but you should have never said them to criminals in a jail."

In the 1920s it was decided that a new jail and courthouse would be built far from the Loop at Twenty-Sixth and California. Cook County Board president Anton Cermak, in whose district the complex would be built, largely influenced the decision. When it opened in 1929, it was considered already obsolete, with inadequate heating and no separate facilities for women. But over the next two decades it provided hundreds of patronage jobs for political bosses. Guards held the lowliest of jobs in the patronage hierarchy at the jail. The only qualification to be a guard was "to get up in the morning and know how to fight," but they were required to do campaign work for their political sponsors. They were grossly underpaid and received little or no formal training. A surprising number of guards could not read or write.

The new jail was also one of a handful of facilities authorized by the State of Illinois to carry out executions. Electrocution had replaced hanging in Illinois on July 6, 1927. The new county jail had a death row and an electric chair in the basement.

The main entrance faces east. An underground tunnel connects it to four unmistakably prisonlike four-story brick-faced buildings behind. The new jail was built to house thirteen hundred prisoners awaiting trial. It was still common for many people in the 1940s to refer to the County Jail as "the Bridewell," after the sixteenth-century palace of Henry VIII that was converted into a notorious London prison. Each floor was divided in tiers consisting of nineteen cells, which were racially segregated until 1949. Each cell had a toilet, was eight feet long, four feet wide, and enclosed with steel bars, and housed two men who slept on bunk beds.

Patrol wagons came and went all day, ferrying prisoners from the city's police stations. During Hickman's stay, prisoners spent as much as fourteen of the twenty-four hours of each day out of their cells. Many would pass the time talking and smoking in the yard, sitting on a wide cement block that according to legend was the foundation for a gallows that was never built. Family and friends visited prisoners on the floors where they were held, but were only allowed to converse through a small opening in a solid steel door. Prisoners met with lawyers in the basement in a large conference room with tables and chairs, and with little privacy. The guards allowed a "Barn Boss" system to reign throughout the jail. The toughest inmate in each tier distributed the meals. Prisoners lined up for breakfast, lunch, and dinner, and the "Barn Boss" would ladle their food from large pots in a "one dip, no lip" manner. The system guaranteed corruption, favoritism, and intimidation among the prisoners.

There was little privacy when Myer met with Hickman in the basement conference room surrounded by other inmates conferring with their attorneys. They discussed what had happened, and Myer agreed to represent him in the upcoming criminal investigation and trial. Back at the SWP office, Mike Bartell began thinking about putting together a defense campaign for James Hickman. He sat down with Bob Birchman, a regular writer for the SWP's newspaper the *Militant*, and Frank Fried, a young navy veteran active in the American Veterans Committee (AVC), a liberal organization. Bartell wanted Birchman to obtain an interview with Hickman as soon as possible, and he asked Fried to start putting out feelers to identify support for Hickman among veterans and union activists.

Soon after the story broke in the *Tribune*, the *Defender* requested an interview with Hickman. This was a great opportunity to get the story out, but it also presented potential problems, as prosecutors also read newspapers. Myer encouraged Hickman to speak to the *Defender*. "Grieving Dad of Tots Shoots Landlord, Tells Police Wounded Man Admitted Setting Fatal West Side Blaze" was the title of the *Defender*'s story. It hit the streets on the weekend of July 19. Speaking from his heart to the *Defender* reporter through a small opening in the steel door of his cell, Hickman had told him that his family had lived "like rats in a hole" in Coleman's building. He had no regrets about shooting Coleman because he "bled us nearly to death" and because tenants' attempts to take Coleman to court always failed. "Every time they would try his case, it was thrown out," Hickman declared. The surviving members of his family were still suffering. His wife and son were still in considerable pain from the injuries they had received from leaping from the burning building. "They are still in misery from that fire. I shall never forget it." Hickman told the reporter that Coleman had confessed to setting the fire after he shot him the first time. "When he thought I was going to kill him. It must have been a death statement."

The charges Hickman would face depended on whether Coleman lived or died. Myer was eager to learn of Coleman's condition. He got his answer on July 19, the same day the *Defender* interview with Hickman appeared, when it was announced that David Coleman had died at Cook County Hospital.

His body was sent to the morgue, where Dr. J. J. Kearns, the same pathologist who had performed the autopsies on the Hickman children, examined it. He measured Coleman's height at five feet, ten inches, his weight at 185 pounds; his age was twenty-five. Sylvestra Coleman filled in an identification form for the coroner's office, where she reported that the last time she had seen her husband alive was at 10:00 p.m. on July 18, 1947, the night before he died. Kearns recovered two .25-caliber copper bullets from Coleman's body during the autopsy. A bullet that had passed through his neck had caused a third wound; this third bullet was still somewhere at the crime scene or in the hands of the police. Kearns noted that Coleman's left lung was filled with blood and that there was extensive organ damage to the lungs, liver, kidneys, and spleen. "In my opinion the death was the result of bullet wounds of the neck," Kearns concluded in his report to the coroner's office.

A coroner's inquest was scheduled for two days later at the county morgue. Mike Myer needed to get a look at the evidence the police had and the case they would make against Hickman. To take full advantage of the expected press coverage of the inquest, he prepared a statement summarizing the background of the case and the formation of a defense committee.

The "Inquest upon the Body of David Coleman" was called to order on July 21, 1947, a cloudy, mild summer day, at the Cook County Morgue by Deputy Coroner Eugene Ingles. Ingles had been present at the four hearings into the deaths of the Hickman children. It must have been very jarring for him to look into the hearing room and see James Hickman sitting there months later, facing a probable murder charge. Ingles announced that Mrs. Sylvestra Coleman, the wife of the deceased, had identified the body as David Coleman. She told the jury that she had been married to David Coleman for two years and that they had two children who were two and three years old.

When Ingles asked whether she knew anything regarding the circumstances leading to the death of her husband, she told him she did not. Irritated that Coleman's wife claimed to know nothing about the fire that killed the Hickman children, Ingles tersely asked her step down and "have a seat over there for the time being."

Ingles called to the stand Chicago police officer John A. Nevelle, who recounted the events of July 16, 1947. Nevelle acknowledged that the police were aware that there had been a fire on January 16 but made no mention of the deaths of the Hickman children. Nevelle wanted the death of Coleman to be treated as the consequence of a straightforward dispute over money.

"He [Hickman] came over at this time to obtain the hundred dollars that he had paid to this fellow [Coleman], that Coleman says, 'I don't owe you any money,' and began shooting." Nevelle failed to mention that in his confession to the police Hickman had reported that he had accused Coleman of starting the fire at 1733 West Washburne and that Coleman had confessed to it.

Myer chose not to question Nevelle. He knew that his testimony would largely reflect the statements of Sylvestra Coleman, Charles McLaurin, and Percy Brown. Brown then took the stand. When Myer got the opportunity to question him, he wanted to get into the official record that Brown's and Hickman's accounts of that day differed significantly.

"Did you hear Coleman say to Mr. Hickman that he had set fire to the house at 1733 Wasburne Avenue?"

"No, Sir."

"Was there any conversation, were they doing any talking before you heard him?"

"No, Sir."

"You heard all the conversation?"

"Every bit of it."

"All you heard was Hickman saying, 'I came after the hundred dollars'?"

"Yes, Sir."

"And then he started shooting?"

"Yes, Sir."

At this point Myer was not aware that during his questioning by John Nevelle at the Third District police station immediately following the shooting, Brown had reported in his sworn statement that Hickman had said more than this.

"What did James Hickman mean," Nevelle had asked Percy at the police station, "when you said he leaned into the car and said to David Coleman, 'they did not make away with you in court'?"

"I reckon he meant that they did not send David Coleman to the Bridewell."

"Why should they send David Coleman to the Bridewell?"

"Well about last January 1947 it seems as Mr. Hickman obtained a lease for a flat at 1733 W. Washburne Ave from. . . . David Coleman, and the building caught on fire, on the fourth floor in the north end, and people got burned and died, that is some children. I don't know whether they belonged to Mr. Hickman or not, and David was arrested at the time. *All the people in the building thought that David Coleman had set the building on fire.*"

James Hickman then took the stand, whereupon Ingles informed him that he did not have to testify and that anything he said could be used against him. Myer told Ingles, "On the advice of counsel, he will not testify." Ingles declared the hearing over and asked the jury to deliberate on a verdict. The jury took a short break and then returned and announced its verdict: "That the said occurrence [the death of Coleman] was murder and recommend that the said James W. Hickman be held to the grand jury." Once Cook County state's attorney William J. Touhy scheduled a grand jury hearing on the death of Coleman, it was almost a certainty that Hickman would be indicted for first-degree murder. Immediately following the closing of the hearing, Hickman was handcuffed and returned to County Jail.

Mike Myer held a press conference outside the coroner's hearing room and made the following statement:

> In Hickman's mind all evidence pointed to Coleman's responsibility for the burning to death of his four children. This idea has obsessed him until it reached the point where he could no longer control himself. At the bottom of this case are the terrible housing conditions under which human beings are compelled to live and particularly the Negroes whose situation is even worse because they are compelled to live in restricted areas. The blame for this killing, as for the death of the four Hickman children, lies squarely on the inhuman housing conditions under which the Negroes are compelled to live.
>
> I have been informed that some progressive organizations and individuals are taking steps to form a committee to aid Mr. Hickman's defense.

On August 1, 1947, the Cook County Grand Jury ruled that James Hickman with "malice aforethought by shooting did kill and murder David Coleman contrary to the Statute, and against the peace and dignity of the State of Illinois." Cook County state's attorney Touhy signed the indictment and soon after announced that Samuel Freeman, one of his most experienced prosecutors, would lead the case.

According to the Illinois Criminal Code of the time,

> Murder is the unlawful killing of a human being, in the peace of the people, with malice aforethought, either expressed or implied. The unlawful killing may be perpetrated by poisoning, striking, starving, drowning, stabbing, shooting, or by any other of the various forms or means by which human nature may be overcome, and death thereby occasioned. Express malice is that deliberate intention unlawfully to take away the life of a fellow creature, which is manifested by external circumstances capable of proof. Malice shall be implied when no considerable provocation appears, or when all the circumstances of the killing show an abandoned and malignant heart.

Punishment for those found guilty was clearly defined:

> Whoever is guilty of murder, shall suffer the punishment of death, or imprisonment in the penitentiary for his natural life, or for a term not less than fourteen years. If the accused is found guilty by a jury, they shall fix the punishment by their verdict; upon a plea of guilty, the punishment shall be fixed by the court.

Did James Hickman have a "malignant heart"? Was there "no considerable provocation" in the shooting of Coleman? Mike Myer would have to address these issues, and anything else that the prosecution would throw at him, if he were to successfully mount a defense of Hickman in the courtroom. Would Freeman ask for the death penalty?

While Hickman was locked up in the County Jail and the State of Illinois prepared its case against him, Mike Bartell mulled over what a defense for Hickman would look like. He was thinking big—something that would really shake up the city. Sitting at his desk drinking coffee, he began thinking about which labor leaders, civil rights activists, actors, actresses, writers, and academics should be involved. He didn't think the campaign would be confined to Chicago; it would have to be national, even international in scope.

In the recent past, SWP had gotten John Dewey, the country's preeminent philosopher, to support Leon Trotsky, and James T. Farrell,

Chicago's best-known fiction writer, to campaign in support of the SWP leaders indicted for sedition. Could such people be enlisted in a campaign for James Hickman's freedom? There was much to do. Where to begin?

Hickman appeared in criminal court on August 6 and pled not guilty to murdering David Coleman and assault with intent to commit murder against Percy Brown. A trial would likely take place in the next eight to twelve weeks.

"My feelings was that I was mistreated without cause."

9

Free James Hickman

The year 1947 turned out to be the one that Willard Motley had been waiting for all his life. His novel *Knock on Any Door* was a best seller. A powerful story of an altar boy who grows up to become a killer, it was a literary sensation. Charles Lee in the *New York Times Book Review* called Motley "an extraordinary and powerful new naturalistic talent" and a "disciple of Dreiser," though Lee cautioned Motley that he still had a good "deal of graduate work to do in literature's school of realism before attaining all the honors of his craft." In Motley's hometown of Chicago, the author and sociologist Horace Cayton, writing in the *Chicago Daily Tribune*, put Motley in the circle of writers who had chronicled the struggles of many migrant groups to attain "the American Way of Life" in the great Midwestern metropolis: "James Farrell described it for the Irish, Nelson Algren for the Polish, Meyer Levin for the Jews, and Richard Wright for the Negroes. Now Willard Motley deals with the Italians. Only he has dealt in such detail with the nuances of human feeling—the delicate balance between love and hate, cruelty and kindness—which exist in the human personality." The *Chicago Defender*, where Motley had once been a youthful columnist writing as Bud Billiken, boasted that "Willard Motley with his first book emerges as an important writer who ranks with the best in the field of fiction." Motley was not content to just attain literary success. Like the much better known Chicagoan Richard Wright, he wanted to use his platform as a writer to fight for social justice. When the opportunity presented itself, he jumped wholeheartedly into the campaign to free James Hickman.

Born in 1909 and raised in the Englewood neighborhood on the South Side of Chicago, Willard Francis Bryant Motley had aspired from a young age to be a writer. As a teen, he wrote the children's "Bud Billiken" column in the *Chicago Defender* for a little over a year, between December 1922 and January 1924. The Englewood he grew up in was a predominantly German and Irish American middle-class neighborhood. The Motleys must have stood out as one of the few Black families in the community, but Willard Motley made no reference to having suffered any overt discrimination or violence while growing up there.

He was raised a Roman Catholic and served as an altar boy at a local church. His familiarity with church rituals and sacraments was later evident in his description of the early life of the main character of *Knock on Any Door*, Nick Romano. In high school he went out for football despite being "a little runt of 133 pounds" whom the bigger players pushed around. He stayed on the team and earned his varsity letter. He also edited a local community house newspaper, the *Cheerleader*. Later in life Motley remembered high school as some of the "happiest days" of his life.

Behind this seemingly normal young adulthood, however, lurked deceit, betrayal, and religious hypocrisy. Sometime during his teenage years he discovered that his pious parents were in fact his grandparents, and that his estranged sister Florence (Flossie) was actually his mother. His biological father was a former boarder at the Motley home, and he and his younger sister, Rita, were products of an illicit affair. All of this had been covered up. Willard never knew his biological father, who disappeared, and Flossie never accepted him as her son. Motley never publicly acknowledged this tortured family history and went along with the cover-up for the rest of his life. The traumatic revelation, however, seems to have been a turning point in his life. It opened up a whole series of questions about family, gender roles, sexuality, and living with lies for appearance's sake. He began to see himself as an outcast and later as an advocate for those on the margins of society.

Motley had an adventurous spirit. He couldn't afford to go to college, but soon after he graduated from Englewood High School in 1929, he began a series of cross-country trips. He wanted to see the world, but he first had to get to New York, where he would take a ship to Europe. He bought a bicycle for three dollars, fastened a sign to it that read "The Knight-Errant of Englewood—Chicago to New York or Bust!" and with fifty-one cents in his pocket started out for New York. Choosing to call himself a knight in search of adventure revealed his romantic notions about himself and his quest.

He covered over one thousand miles in thirteen days, sleeping in such places as a jail cell, a graveyard, and a church basement along the way before arriving in New York. He never made it to Europe, though, and instead returned to Chicago. He turned his curiosity to nearby states, traveling by car around the Midwest and eventually the West. He began earning a small income as a travel writer. Many of the people he met on his travels provided raw material for his later novels.

During this time away from home, he must have pondered the revelations about his family history. Questions about his own sexuality must have surfaced. According to Motley's close friends, he was gay, but this was revealed to only a small circle of people. His time away from his watchful family while traveling from one city to another must have provided him with opportunities to explore his sexuality.

By the late 1930s, Motley was back in Chicago and settled in the Maxwell Street neighborhood just southwest of the Loop, one of the city's few polyglot neighborhoods where various ethnic and racial groups lived in close proximity. The famed outdoor Maxwell Street Market—selling everything imaginable—stretched for many blocks, crowded with tens of thousands of shoppers on weekends. The market was a lively place, its air filled with the barking sounds of pitchmen. "Pullers" on the sidewalks would try to entice shoppers into the stores, touting their latest sale. Customers would aggressively bargain with sellers. It was something of the Old World in the heart of modern Chicago, a city that had virtually invented the department store. Motley lived for many years in the neighborhood and kept a close eye on the people and dynamics of the community. It is here that *Knock on Any Door* is set.

Motley helped launch the *Hull House Magazine* in 1939, and the following year he started working for the Federal Writers Project of the Works Project Administration, the New Deal program that supported writers during the Depression. With the approach of the Second World War, Motley began to take militant positions on political issues that would be characteristic of his views for the rest of his life.

In 1940, a year after war had broken out in Europe, the Selective Training and Service Act was passed by Congress and signed into law by President Roosevelt. It was the first peacetime draft in US history and continued the long-standing practice, despite protests from civil rights groups, of racial segregation in all branches of the US military. Declaring that he would not serve in a Jim Crow military, Motley filed for and received conscientious objector status. His interest in radical politics increased. In 1942, he started hosting classes of the Communist Party's Workers School at his apartment, and the following year he took out a subscription to its newspaper, the *Daily Worker*. But his positions on the war and the draft were at odds with the Communist Party's positions, and he never joined.

While working as a lab technician, Motley spent the war years writing *Knock on Any Door*. Originally over one thousand pages in length, it was edited to roughly half that size before it was released in early May 1947. *Knock on Any Door* is a unique book by an African American writer because its drama revolves around the struggles of white people, the Romano family. Thrown from a comfortable middle-class existence into desperate straits by the Depression, the Romanos are forced to move their favorite son, the altar boy Nick, to a much tougher school and neighborhood, where he is arrested and convicted of a minor crime that he didn't commit. The reform school to which he is sent to is a living hell and only deepens his distrust and hatred of society's institutions. After reform school, he and his family leave their hometown of Denver and move to Chicago's Maxwell Street neighborhood in the hopes of finding a better life. The situation gets worse for Nick, however, as he is attracted to the dark side of city life and runs afoul of a sadistic cop, Riley, whom he kills in a gun battle. He is tried, found guilty of murder, and sentenced to death. At every point, Romano's tragic life is shaped by institutional failure. By the novel's climax, Motley's opposition to the death penalty comes across clearly and eloquently.

Knock on Any Door quickly became a best seller in 1947, selling more than 47,000 copies during its first three weeks on the market and 350,000 over the next two years. Motley's many years of writing in obscurity had come to an end. The novel appealed to a large audience that was concerned about both juvenile delinquency and life in America's crooked "Second City."

To some, Motley's deep brown eyes and arching eyebrows gave him a world-weary look. An entertaining and captivating speaker, he was in great demand to speak about his novel throughout that year. He spoke at a variety of conferences, community meetings, and clubs and was honored by many organizations. The Society of Midland Authors held a reception for him in early May 1947. It was his first public appearance since the novel's release. The reception was cosponsored by the Mayor's Commission on Human Relations, the Parkway Community House, the National Conference of Christians and Jews, the Anti-Defamation League, and the Chicago Council against Racial and Religious Discrimination. This was followed by other speaking engagements and tributes by the Friends of the Negro Writer and the Chicago College Club. Motley spoke at the Midwestern Writers' annual conference together with another rising Chicago author, Nelson Algren. Hollywood producer David O. Selznick purchased the movie rights to the novel in October, and it was initially rumored that Marlon Brando was going to play the lead. The film was made in 1949 and starred Humphrey Bogart, with John Derek playing Nick Romano.

Motley was the type of public figure that Mike Bartell hoped to get involved in the Hickman defense campaign. But first he needed someone who would be willing to do the "Jimmy Higgins" work of the defense committee: answer the phones and the mail, go to endless meetings, work long hours with little or no pay—the day-in, day-out work that glues a campaign together. He had one person in mind.

Frank Fried had just gotten out of the US Navy at the beginning of 1947. He was twenty years old and was trying to figure out what he was going to do with the rest of his life. He found himself hanging around the SWP office, waiting for something to come along that would excite him. When Bartell told him that the SWP was going to mount a defense campaign for James Hickman and needed someone to work full time on it, he eagerly accepted.

Bartell and Fried sat down and brainstormed about who should be invited to an initial planning meeting to form the Hickman defense committee. Bartell wanted a small, quick meeting of like-minded people who would focus on preparing an open letter appealing for support for Hickman. He insisted that he attend the first meeting, but after that he wanted to play a behind-the-scenes role in the campaign. If the campaign were to really take off, it would have to include important figures from the Chicago labor and civil rights movements, or it could be dismissed as the fringe effort of a marginal radical group.

Fried contacted Sidney Lens and asked whether he would be interested in hosting campaign meetings at his office. Lens readily agreed.

Born Sidney Okun in 1912 in Newark, New Jersey, he was the son of Charles and Sophie Okun. "I changed my surname to Lens in the mid-1930s when I was blacklisted for union activity and couldn't find a job under my own name," he wrote in his autobiography *Unrepentant Radical* many decades later. His parents were Russian Jews who had arrived in the United States in 1907. Lens's father, like Mike Myer's, was a refugee from the Russian military draft. He died when Lens was three years old from cirrhosis of the liver, an illness that is usually the product of extreme alcoholism. His mother had made a harrowing escape from Russia before her husband. Sophie was part of a group escaping across the border led by a "border runner" who kept yelling at one woman in the group to stop her baby from crying. "The child was dead, my mother said, by the time they reached safety."

Lens's mother settled in New York City after his father died, and worked a sixty-four-hour week in New York City's garment district. Lens graduated from high school at seventeen and went to work on Wall Street as a runner in a brokerage firm. Soon after the stock market crash of 1929, he lost his job. He tried his hand at being a writer and a playwright, but without much success. He couldn't escape the larger issues of the world that began to press on his mind: the Depression, fascism, war. "One could no longer languish in the luxury of disengagement. I made up my mind to join a leftist group, the only question being whether it would be the Communists or Trotskyites."

He gorged himself on books, reading Trotsky's monumental *History of the Russian Revolution* and other articles and pamphlets critical of the Communist Party. In late 1934, he made up his mind and joined the Trotskyist Communist League of America (CLA). "It was an exhilarating feeling, assuaging a sense of guilt that I had stayed on the sidelines while others had made the commitment. The simple act of joining had a certain finality to it, washing away doubts and indecision. I was on a one-way trip toward a beautiful tomorrow." But a little more than a year later he and several dozen others refused to join the Socialist Party with the rest of the Trotskyist movement. They founded a small organization called the Revolutionary Workers League (RWL) with a newspaper, the *Fighting Worker.*

Lens's life was typical of the young radicals of that generation. He estimated that he hitchhiked at least forty or fifty thousand miles from 1935 to 1940, looking for the next exciting thing to get involved in, whether it be fighting for the unemployed or organizing taxicab drivers. During his first sojourn to Chicago in 1936, Lens found himself in a high-profile clash with city hall. In early July, the city had stopped providing cash relief to eighty-three thousand families, throwing them into a desperate situation. The Illinois Workers Alliance (IWA), one of major organizations of the unemployed, immediately called for a mass demonstration at city hall to put pressure on Mayor Ed Kelly and the aldermen. Lens and a dozen RWL members got to city hall first and began picketing with signs that read "Nationalization of Industry under Workers Control" and "Jobs at Trade Union Wages." Hundreds of members and supporters of the IWA joined the picket line, pushed their way past the police, and took over the visitors' galleries above the shocked aldermen and mayor. "For a while there was pandemonium," the *Chicago Daily Tribune* reported. "A blond youth [Lens] and a Negro girl began to make speeches." Lens denounced the council for its callous action. Mayor Kelly scrambled to save the situation. "It was a great victory," Lens later recalled. "The council, which had claimed it didn't have any money, somehow raised the funds to send out food boxes that were six days overdue, that very day."

After several years of being a footloose radical, Lens decided to settle in Chicago and focus on union organizing in the retail industry. He got a job in 1941 at Hillmans, one of the larger grocery store chains in the Chicago area, whose employees were represented, or more accurately robbed and terrorized, by Local 1248 of the AFL's Retail Clerks' International Protective Association, led by Max Caldwell. Caldwell was an old-fashioned labor gangster whose usual method of "organizing" was to tell prospective union members to join and pay dues or "you'll get your legs broken." Caldwell signed sweetheart deals with the bosses. Lens managed to get a critical mass of his coworkers to switch their support to Local 329 of the Retail, Wholesale, and Department Store Union (associated with the CIO).

This was no mean feat. Caldwell was a hefty, menacing thug in league with the heirs of Al Capone's criminal empire. Lens was soon elected to lead his local union. In 1946, Lens, feeling that his little local union didn't have enough influence, led Local 329 out of the CIO and into the AFL's Building Service Employees International Union, which had a firmer footing in Chicago's retail giants. Outside of his job as a union official, his political activity became "scattershot in the sense that they were not related to one another, but were done solely for a good cause." He began to fear that the radical era that had shaped his life was coming to an end, but he was determined to use his position in the labor movement for good causes. "This first one of major importance was the Hickman case," he recalled four decades later.

After learning that Lens had joined the Hickman defense committee, Bartell called Willoughby Abner, whom he had gotten to know extremely well since moving to Chicago. Abner was president of UAW Local 734. A tall man with a broad smile and a charismatic personality, he was emerging as a leading Black trade unionist in Chicago and was a prominent supporter of UAW president Walter Reuther. He was also very ambitious. Abner wanted to use the power of organized labor to tear apart Jim Crow racism and transform the political landscape. He was an active member of the Chicago NAACP.

Born in Chicago on December 6, 1920, Abner had spent a few years of his youth in Detroit but had returned to Chicago. During the Second World War, he organized thousands of workers into the UAW in several South Side foundries and manufacturing facilities. Abner had obtained a law degree from the John Marshall Law School in 1947 but didn't take the bar exam; he wanted to be a political figure, not a lawyer. Though interested in radical ideas (he attended many SWP public forums on a wide variety of issues), he did not join the party, unlike his close friend Charles Chiakulas, who had joined in 1947.

Chiakulas was president of UAW Local 477 and worked at Revere Copper and Brass, a Northwest Side company that traced its roots back to the American revolutionary Paul Revere. After organizing Revere Copper's fifteen hundred workers into the UAW, he moved on to organizing truck and auto parts factories throughout the Chicago area. Chiakulas had a rough-and-tumble public image earned on the picket line that hid a political sophistication underneath.

Things were moving fast. On August 6 James Hickman was arraigned for the murder of David Coleman and for assault with intent to commit murder against Percy Brown. He pleaded not guilty to both charges. A trial date was set for Monday, September 29. The planning meeting for the Hickman campaign was held two days later at Sidney Lens's office in Chicago's Loop. Mike Bartell, Frank Fried, Sidney Lens, Bill Abner, and Charles Chiakulas were joined by Bernis Johnson, vice president of the West Side Youth Council, one of the young civil rights activists Bartell had met during the course of tenant organizing on the West Side. They had less than eight weeks to build a campaign before the first trial date.

Bartell suggested that a letter appealing for support for Hickman be addressed to the city's most progressive labor and civil rights leaders and activists. All agreed. The appeal would also set the time and place for a meeting to create a defense committee that would elect officers and decide on a plan of action. Bartell agreed to write a draft of the appeal, and it went out the next day. It recounted the basic facts of the case and made a pitch for getting involved in the defense campaign: "All of us are duty bound to help in the defense of James Hickman. The undersigned civic and labor leaders are sponsoring the establishment of a City-wide Defense Committee to aid in the defense of Mr. Hickman. You, as an outstanding person in civic affairs, can be of invaluable assistance in this work. We are therefore extending you an invitation to attend a dinner meeting for the purpose of setting up the defense committee."

Willoughby Abner, Charles Chiakulas, and Bernis Johnson signed the letter, along with the last-minute additions of Dr. James Luther Adams and Reverend Joseph Evans. Adams was a professor at the Meadville Theological School, affiliated with the University of Chicago, and a well-known activist around issues of racial and religious discrimination in Chicago. Evans was pastor of the Metropolitan Community Church on the South Side, one of the most important venues for civil rights organizing in the Black community.

At the meeting held the following week at the YMCA in the Loop, Abner, Chiakulas, and Bernice Howard of the NAACP were elected chairman, treasurer, and secretary respectively of the newly formed Hickman Defense Committee. An executive committee was also elected, made up of Adams, Evans, Lens, Fried, Gerald Bullock of CORE, and Miles Cartman of the NAACP. They voted to organize a mass rally in support of Hickman at the Metropolitan Community Church on Sunday afternoon, September 28—the day before the beginning of Hickman's trial.

The whole strategy of the Hickman defense campaign was to bring enough public pressure, according to Fried, to "make it politically impossible in the eyes of the people of Chicago for the prosecutors to convict Hickman." The campaign would combine street-level organizing with articles in the local press, newspaper advertising, and public rallies. "We put a collection can for donations, a petition, and leaflets about Hickman in every store, bar, or restaurant we could in the Black neighborhoods in Chicago," Fried recalled, describing the early days of the campaign. "People gave generously. Everybody knew about Hickman. I think the prosecution was screwed from the beginning."

Bartell asked SWP member Bob Birchman to write an article on the Hickman case for the SWP's magazine *Fourth International.* In "The Case of James Hickman," Birchman outlined the facts of the case and the reasons, in his opinion, for there being broad support for Hickman in Chicago's Black community. "Every so often a previously unknown individual suddenly attracts wide attention. There is usually a social reason for this. The story connected with the particular case epitomizes the plight of voiceless millions, focusing on the needs of one group and the crimes of another . . . Hickman's story is the story of Jim Crow as it is practiced north of the Mason-Dixon line." James Hickman, a "previously unknown individual," had become a social symbol for Black Chicagoans.

In the weeks that followed, Bartell became increasingly impressed with Fried's hard work. He was "a real sparkplug," Bartell reported to the SWP's national office in New York. Fried was a young man of medium height and stocky build with bluish green eyes that sparkled during political debate and discussion. Despite his youth, he had accumulated enough political experience in a few short years to be an effective campaign organizer.

Born in Chicago on March 1, 1927, Franklin Edwin Fried was the son of Walter and Bertha Fried. His mother had been born in Hungary and his father in the United States; he had one older sister, Vivian. Walter was a lawyer who aspired to be a judge. Although Walter stayed in the right wing of the Democratic Party, everyone in his family loved Franklin Roosevelt. The Frieds were Jewish, but they were very secular and Americanized. "My parents were very Waspy Jews," Frank Fried recalled later. While they were somewhat shielded from the worst aspects of the Depression in its early years, it ultimately shaped their lives and aspirations. Like so many others, the Frieds lived one short step from disaster. In 1936 Walter died and the family finances were wiped out. "We went from three of us living in a seven-room apartment to living in a three-room apartment. It was difficult for my mother to support us, so I was sent to an orphanage, then to a military academy," Frank Fried explained later.

"I was always interested in politics," Fried said about his teenage years. When the economy began to revive, he returned home to live with his mother in Hyde Park, a largely middle-class neighborhood in Chicago's South Side. Hyde Park's wide, tree-lined streets, large apartments, and easy access to Lake Michigan made it one of Chicago's more desirable neighborhoods, despite its proximity to the stockyards. It was the home of the University of Chicago, with its pseudo-Gothic architecture modeled on that of the many centuries older University of Oxford.

Fried attended the university for one year starting in 1943. During the 1930s, the University of Chicago had been one of the main bastions of student radicalism in the country. The Communist Party was the most important radical group on campus; it led antiwar strikes, fights against racism, and campaigns in support of civil liberties and the CIO. The radical presence on campus continued into the 1940s. But after the United States entered the war a strange role reversal took place: the Communist Party became one of the most patriotic groups on campus and abandoned most of the campaigns that had made its reputation. Many of the other socialists on campus also supported the war but not to the same self-destructive extent as the Communist Party.

"Politically, I was fresh meat for the Communist Party, but the local organizer turned me off," Fried recalled. One of the first socialists Fried met on campus told him how Roosevelt was persecuting socialists for violating the Smith Act. "I said that's not my Roosevelt." He soon discovered that it *was* his Roosevelt, however, and joined the Socialist Party's youth group, the Young People's Socialist League. He also joined the Labor Rights Society on campus. It had only fifteen members, but they were eager to get their hands dirty supporting the labor movement. They got their chance with the Montgomery Ward strike.

"It was one of those struggles that are bigger than life," Fried recalled many decades later, "when the radicals' dreams fuse with the workers' own aspirations and things get really heady." Montgomery Ward was the mail-order giant based in Chicago. Its founder, Aaron Montgomery Ward, had revolutionized the retail business beginning in 1872 by selling goods directly to customers through his catalog, bringing thousands of goods into the homes of people who couldn't shop at department stores in the big cities. Ward promised "satisfaction or your money back." It was a huge success.

In 1908, Montgomery Ward built a huge, multibuilding warehousing and office complex for its burgeoning empire along the north branch of the Chicago River. The warehouses contained miles of chutes, conveyors, and storage lofts where thousands of workers processed and filled orders that would be delivered by the post office across the country. A four-story tower with a pyramidal roof was added to the company headquarters in 1929, crowned with a 22.5-foot bronze statue that had originally adorned its headquarters on Michigan Avenue, a symbol of Ward's managers' confidence in themselves and the firm's future.

Success bred arrogance and a hatred for trade unions. The retail industry as a whole was particularly resistant to trade unions in the 1930s and '40s. Montgomery Ward employed nearly sixty thousand workers across the country during the Second World War. Even though it was not directly tied to the war effort, it came under the jurisdiction of the War Labor Board (WLB), the mammoth wartime agency that oversaw labor relations in the United States. Sewell Avery, the sixty-nine-year-old head of the company and longtime opponent of Roosevelt's New Deal, had previously signed WLB-supervised contracts with a small retail union, the United Retail, Wholesale, Sales & Department Store Employees of America (URWSDE) Local 20, which represented Montgomery Ward's workers in Chicago. Beginning in 1943, Avery provoked a series of confrontations with the union and the WLB that many people in the labor movement saw as harbingers of things to come after the war's end. After he refused to renew a contract with the union, tension built over the next year until the union struck in Chicago. It was the only CIO-sanctioned strike during the war years.

Frank Fried was among a group of about thirty University of Chicago students, organized by the Labor Rights Society, who went to the union's strike headquarters to offer support. "The organizers told us we could help raise money, we could help picket," he later recalled. "We went to work getting University of Chicago students to give money to the strike fund, and we shivered with the picketers in the cold outside Montgomery Ward. Nobody seemed to mind that we were students."

Picketing was particularly important for the strike. Hundreds of strikers confronted the notoriously violent, corrupt, and antiunion Chicago police, who mercilessly beat them. Sidney Lens and Fred Socki, staff organizers with a sister local of the strikers, were assigned to help organize the strike, which became a bitter fight.

On the morning of April 12, 1944, the first day of the strike, thousands of strikers, mostly women, milled around the entrances to the struck warehouse near Chicago Avenue and the north branch of the Chicago River. Lens had been there for several hours when, just as the picket lines were crippling Ward's operations, the police showed up in force. "There was a scuffle, and Captain George Barnes of the Chicago labor detail took a swing at me, missed, and hit Mike Mann—secretary of the Chicago Industrial Union Council—square on the jaw." Many other picketers got the same treatment. Predictably, the infamously conservative and antiunion *Chicago Tribune* led the howling press campaign against the strikers.

The courts came down hard on the strikers, limiting the number of pickets, despite the efforts of Mike Myer and Francis Heisler, who were Local 20's attorneys. Given Avery's open defiance of the WLB, Roosevelt himself ordered the military to seize the plant and the strikers to return to work. Avery remained defiant and was removed from his office, while still sitting in his chair with his arms folded, by two battle-dressed National Guardsmen. The outrageous behavior of Ward's management forced virtually the entire labor movement, including both the AFL and the CIO, to come out in support of the strikers despite formally adhering to a "no-strike" pledge. The notable exceptions were unions led by the Communist Party, which opposed wartime strikes under any circumstances whatsoever.

Despite this support, the union was defeated, as the military left Ward's management in place to terrorize the workforce. Not until many years after the war came to an end were Montgomery Ward's warehouses unionized once again.

The battle at Montgomery Ward was an important turning point for the labor and socialist movement in Chicago. The Communist Party was further diminished in the eyes of many people. Several people who met on the picket line and shared the cuts and bruises meted out by the Chicago police, including Michael Mann, Sidney Lens, and Mike Bartell, would work together again over the coming years.

The strike also drew Frank Fried closer to the Socialist Workers Party. Two days before his eighteenth birthday, on February 27, 1945, he joined the SWP. The next day he joined the US navy. The draft was hanging over his head, and better to be in the navy than cannon fodder in the army, Fried thought at the time. But he later reported hating his eighteen months in the navy. It was petty and boring. Never leaving the continental United States, he was forced to divide his time between the Great Lakes Naval Training Station forty miles north of Chicago and Bremerton, Washington.

After he was discharged, he got a job at International Harvester in Melrose Park, a suburb of Chicago, but it proved even more boring than the navy. He couldn't focus on his job and was soon fired. He joined a local branch of the American Veterans Committee (AVC), founded in 1943, which sought to provide a liberal alternative to the established right-wing veterans organizations like the American Legion and the Veterans of Foreign Wars (VFW). Among the AVC's most prominent members were Franklin Roosevelt Jr., son of the president, and the actor Ronald Reagan, who was then a liberal.

Although the AVC did a lot of good work for returning veterans, it felt a little too respectable and middle class for the professional revolutionary Fried thought himself to be—he was eager to get involved in a real fighting campaign. Mike Bartell had merged the three SWP branches in Chicago into one big citywide branch. There was a separate branch among steelworkers just over the state line in Indiana. To Fried the SWP felt like "a small working-class party." He and Bartell had met each other on the Montgomery Ward picket lines in his prenavy days. But it was during the Hickman defense campaign that they became close friends. Bartell became like an older brother, a mentor, to Fried.

Fried subsisted on roughly ten dollars a week during the entire Hickman campaign and took meals wherever they were offered, sleeping many nights on the office couch. His connection with the AVC proved fruitful—the Chicago Area Council of the AVC signed on as a supporter of the Hickman Defense Committee. He contacted the ACLU, the Civil Liberties Union of Chicago, and Americans for Democratic Action, and they agreed to send out fundraising appeals to their mailing lists.

At the end of August Fried put on his best suit and tie and went to the regularly scheduled meeting of the Baptist Ministers Conference of Chicago, an organization that brought together many mainline African American Baptist churches. Fried laid out the facts of the case before these pastors and closed his presentation with an impassioned plea for support. The ministers, many of whose parishioners struggled in conditions identical to those that the Hickman family had faced, took only a few minutes to decide to sign on as an organizational supporter of the campaign and to take up a collection for Hickman's legal expenses at all of their services the following Sunday. This was quite an important endorsement and showed the depth of support for Hickman throughout the Black community.

Fried hit the road and traveled through the Midwest, then went east to New York to meet with SWP members and supporters stitching together the beginning of a nationwide network of Hickman defense committees. The focus of the campaign, however, remained in Chicago.

Mike Bartell made a cold call to Willard Motley. He had never met Motley before, but from the newspapers he read voraciously every day he knew about the big buzz surrounding Motley's book. Motley replied that he was definitely interested in supporting the Hickman Defense Committee and asked what he could do. Bartell asked whether he wanted to meet Hickman and write an article about the case. Motley jumped at the chance.

Soon Motley and Bartell met James Hickman in the county jail and later sat down with Annie Hickman. Motley was deeply moved by his meeting with Hickman. He later wrote, "I felt that perhaps I, too, or almost any other man, would have done the same thing as he has done, given the same circumstances." He took detailed notes for a public statement he would write on Hickman's behalf that would be widely circulated in the coming weeks.

Soon afterward, Bartell told Motley that a small delegation of Hickman Defense Committee activists was going to be meeting with Marshall Field III and asked whether he wanted to come along. Field was the heir to the Marshall Field Department Store fortune and the editor and publisher of the *Chicago Sun*, liberal rival to the conservative *Chicago Daily Tribune*. Field had spent much of his youth in England attending the famous institutions of the British aristocracy, Eaton and Cambridge University. He had fought in the First World War and returned to the United States to pursue various business interests. He was very rich, an Anglophile, and a Republican. The Depression and the New Deal constituted a turning point in his life, however, and he became an active liberal and supporter of FDR.

Having become interested in newspaper publishing, he bankrolled the founding of the New York daily *PM* starting in 1940 and the *Chicago Sun* in 1941. Field was one of the few major publishers Bartell thought could be approached about joining the campaign for Hickman's freedom. A few days before the Hickman supporters sat down with Field, the *Chicago Sun* ran an article announcing that the Chicago Industrial Union Council of the CIO had given its full support to Hickman. Willoughby Abner, the principal actor behind the council's actions, promised that he would "put in motion its entire machinery in support of the Hickman Defense Committee." The *Sun* went on to announce the mass rally scheduled on the eve of Hickman's trial at the Metropolitan Community Church.

Bartell, Lens, and Motley were optimistic about Field's support when they were ushered into his office. Having listened to their pitch, Field agreed to print the press releases of the Hickman Defense Committee. But he balked at donating space for Motley's appeal for Hickman's freedom. When they said the committee would pay for the space, Field still said no, he would not print it. The meeting ended quickly. Motley was infuriated by Field's decision. He stewed with an anger that exploded two weeks later at the mass rally. Shut out of the *Sun* and other Chicago dailies, the defense committee turned to the next best possibility.

Leo Lerner was a major partner in a chain of neighborhood newspapers throughout the Chicago area. "A fistfight on Clark Street is more important to our readers than a war in Europe"—so went a saying attributed to him. Born and raised in Chicago, he was a well-known liberal and active in Americans for Democratic Action. By the late 1940s, the sixteen weekly neighborhood newspapers of the Caplan-Lerner Home Newspapers chain had a total circulation of about 219,000. Lerner's weeklies may have been the little cousins to the big dailies, but they reached into the same working-class and middle-class urban and suburban communities from which a jury pool would be drawn.

After Lerner was told that Marshall Field wouldn't publish Motley's appeal, he gladly opened the pages of his newspapers. Boasting that it was an "exclusive in the Caplan-Lerner Home Newspapers," the *North Town News* declared in bolt print, "Willard Motley Tells Hickman Story," alongside a photo of James and Annie with three of their children who died in the fire. Motley didn't hold back his feelings about the case in his twelve-hundred-word appeal:

> You have seen many pictures of men who have killed. You have seen the photographs of the returned soldier. Perhaps next door lives a boy who killed some other boy during the war. In the war, millions of men killed other millions of men because they believed they were a threat to their homes, their wives, their children. This threat was thousands of miles from home. These were strangers killed, with whom there had been no personal contact.
>
> James Hickman killed the man who had threatened his wife and children with a death more horrible than the Nazi gas chambers. And carried it out. This is what I was thinking of as I sat talking to Hickman today. Hickman needs help. There are three children left who need him. A wife who needs him. Will you help us help him?

Motley's appeal was sent to Black newspapers across the country and was also printed in the September 13, 1947, edition of the *Chicago Defender* under the headline "Motley Cites Another Unwritten Law in Defense of James Hickman." This raised the profile of the case immensely and virtually guaranteed a huge turnout for the rally at the Metropolitan Community Church. More important, it laid out the case for Hickman in such a persuasive manner that it was hard to read it and not be convinced that a great injustice was taking place.

At the same time, Lens had been writing and talking to everyone he knew about the Hickman campaign. He wanted the broadest possible support for Hickman before the trial began. The executive committee of the Hickman Defense Committee decided to create an advisory board for the campaign made up of sympathetic well-known public figures who, although not involved in the day-to-day decision making of the campaign, could speak, write, or contribute in some other way to it. Lens and others recruited many distinguished people to the advisory board, including, among others, Jacob Weinstein, rabbi of the oldest synagogue in the Midwest; Truman Gibson Jr., one of the organizers of the American Negro Exposition in 1940, which marked the seventy-fifth anniversary of Emancipation, and a former official in the War Department who investigated grievances of Black soldiers during the Second World War; Michael Mann of the CIO Industrial Union Council; and Carl Reiner, the comedian and Broadway entertainer.

It was an impressive list, organized in a short space of time. Lens was feeling good about the upcoming rally but still felt that someone who could definitely bring out a crowd was needed. Tallulah Bankhead was just the right person. She had become famous on Broadway as a stage actress and was a perennial favorite of society reporters, who could always count on her for a controversial quote or two. A few years earlier she had starred in Alfred Hitchcock's *Lifeboat*, her most famous screen performance. Currently she was starring in Noël Coward's *Private Lives* at a theater in Chicago. Lens's office was near the theater district in the Loop. "I was leaving my office on Dearborn Street one evening," he later remembered, "when I noticed her name on the marquee half a block away. She was starring in a new play. On the spur of the moment, I went to the stage door and asked for her. To my surprise, she knew about Hickman and was immensely sympathetic. When I asked her, however, to speak at the rally we planned at the Metropolitan Community Church, she shuddered as if I had hit her with a blast of arctic air. 'Why, Mr. Lens, how can I make a speech?' It took a little while to figure out that what she meant was she was capable of reciting other people's lines, but she was incapable of constructing a speech of her own."

Lens agreed to write a speech for her. He wrote a rough draft and had it delivered to the theater. A couple of days later she told him, "I read it to my secretary and made her cry. I'll be happy to deliver it." But dealing with a star is never easy. Several days before the rally, she contacted Lens's office and left a message saying that she had taken ill and would most likely not attend. Lens was out of town on union business. When he returned, he wrote a note to Bankhead that is a model for handling difficult and mercurial personalities:

> Upon returning from Peoria I was very sorry to hear that you haven't been feeling well lately. I hope that the situation clears up so that you can deliver this short talk. The Negro press has been playing up the meeting for a number of weeks and your appearance at it. Hundreds of posters announcing the event, two sound trucks, 40,000 leaflets, an ad in the Chicago Sun have already publicized your appearance most extensively. This is not in the nature of "soft-soap" or flattery, but I know from my own personal knowledge that innumerable people on the South Side will feel greatly disappointed if you cannot appear.

Of course, it *was* all soft-soap and flattery, with just a hint that it would be bad for Bankhead's public image if she backed out. In addition, Lens made sure that a car picked her up and later took her back to her hotel, and that a copy of the speech was ready for her. Why all the fuss?

Tallaluh Bankhead was one of the most unlikely advocates of racial equality in the United States. She had been born in 1902 into a wealthy aristocratic family in Alabama. Her father, William, would eventually become speaker of the US House of Representatives from 1936 to 1940, during Franklin Roosevelt's second term as president. She was raised in the South during one of the worst eras of race relations in the twentieth century, in the years following the infamous 1896 Supreme Court ruling *Plessy v. Ferguson*, which legalized the American system of apartheid known as Jim Crow. "Separate but equal" became the law of the land, and it was closely intertwined with the disenfranchisement of the Black population and a romanticization of the Old South plantation culture.

Tallulah Bankhead was by all accounts an intelligent, independent, and strong-willed child. After winning a beauty contest when she was fifteen, she moved to New York City to become a stage actor. It wasn't until the late 1930s that she found fame and success in Hollywood—

her breakthrough performance was in *The Little Foxes* (1939), penned by Communist Party sympathizer Lillian Hellman. The play revolves around the fictional southern aristocrat Regina Hubbard Giddens, who struggles for wealth and freedom within the suffocating confines of early twentieth-century Alabama society. Bankhead's stage success spawned a political awakening in her, and a confidence to go public with long-felt but hidden ideas.

She broke with her southern Democratic family's conservatism, particularly its virulent racism, although she remained personally close to her father. Bankhead clearly saw herself as an aristocratic rebel. She also adopted the endearing or annoying (depending on one's point of view) habit of calling everyone "darling"—or as she pronounced it, "*dah*-ling."

Several months after *The Little Foxes* ended its run on Broadway, Bankhead threw herself into organizing the weeklong Fourth Annual National Sharecroppers Awareness Week in New York City in May 1940. Two Socialist Party–allied organizations—the Southern Tenant Farmers Union and the Workers Defense League, its political defense arm—organized this annual event. It was endorsed by a broad array of organizations, and its purpose was to raise awareness and funds for southern sharecroppers who worked in semifeudal conditions and faced state and vigilante violence when they attempted to organize.

Bankhead's father was furious and demanded that she withdraw her name. She did, but then worked behind the scenes with Broadway and Hollywood star Paul Muni (famous for his films *Scarface* and *I Am a Fugitive from a Chain Gang*) and other members of the Sharecroppers Awareness Week theater committee. The week culminated in a huge rally at Madison Square Garden. Among the featured speakers were A. Phillip Randolph of the Brotherhood of Sleeping Car Porters, Walter White and W. E. B. Dubois of the NAACP, David Dubinsky of the International Ladies' Garment Workers' Union, and Norman Thomas of the Socialist Party.

Throughout the 1940s, Bankhead made a point of appearing in interracial casts on stage and screen and supporting Black athletes. (In the summer 1940 Chicago production of *The Little Foxes* she shared the stage with African American actors Abbie Mitchell and John Marriott.) In 1944, as the cynical reporter Constance Porter in Alfred Hitchcock's *Lifeboat*, she shared the screen with Canada Lee, second only to Paul Robeson as the most important Black stage actor in the United States at the time. Lee had played Bigger Thomas in the stage production of Richard Wright's *Native Son*.

Bankhead joined Lee in a fight to stop the extradition of Herman Powell from New Jersey to Georgia. Powell, an African American, had been sentenced to life in prison for the "murder" of a white woman in Georgia as a result of a car accident on a rainy day, in which both he and the woman were severely injured. She died five days after the accident, and Powell was nearly lynched. After serving one year of his life sentence, Powell escaped from prison and fled to New Jersey, where he and his wife lived in peace for two years before local police arrested him. A thirty-month battle ensued, in which Bankhead, Lee, and Robeson, along with Joe Louis, campaigned to stop Powell's extradition. Despite their all-out effort, Powell was sent back to a Georgia chain gang at the end of 1946.

In 1947 Bankhead began her longest tour since *The Little Foxes*, appearing in Coward's *Private Lives*. That summer she was in Chicago and was asked to speak out against lynching. During the previous year, an all-white jury in Greenville, South Carolina, had acquitted twenty-one white men—many of whom had confessed—of the lynching murder of Willie Earle. This incident, along with many others, had given new life to the campaign to pass a federal antilynching bill. Thirty-seven Chicago aldermen urged President Harry Truman to push for passage of the bill. Bankhead spoke on the South Side at a July 1947 rally sponsored by the Chicago Citizens Committee against Lynching; she told five hundred people in the overwhelmingly Black audience that lynching was one of "her pet hates" and described how her father had stopped a lynching when he was a student at the University of Alabama.

It only made sense that Sidney Lens would seek Bankhead's star power to galvanize the rally in support of James Hickman that was organized only two short months later.

The Metropolitan Community Church was located at Forty-First Street and Parkway Avenue (now Martin Luther King Drive) on Chicago's South Side. Its pastor was Reverend Joseph Evans, who had been one of the first people to sign the open letter calling for a defense campaign for James Hickman. The church had been a forum for fighting racism and for labor organizing in Chicago's Black community. In July 1943, the church had hosted the National Conference of the March on Washington Movement led by A. Philip Randolph. Its sanctuary could hold roughly twelve hundred people.

The "Help Free James Hickman" rally was scheduled to begin at 3:00 p.m. on Sunday afternoon after church services. The pews filled up quickly, and with them an atmosphere of tense anticipation. Willoughby Abner was the master of ceremonies. He opened the rally with a rousing speech and introduced the speakers one by one. Willard Motley made an impassioned call to save Hickman's life and denounced liberals like Marshall Field III "who talk out of both sides of their mouths." Mike Myer took off his lawyer's cap and roared to the crowd, "It is not Hickman who should be on trial, but the inhuman landlords and real estate interests who sacrifice human lives for profit, for they are the real criminals." Ralph Helstein, international president of the United Packinghouse Workers of America, and Henry McGee, president of the Chicago branch of the NAACP and a postal worker, both spoke and gave messages of solidarity.

Tallulah Bankhead brought audience members to their feet and, according to Lens, "drew tears from the whole audience" with a riveting speech:

> It seems to me a shameful condemnation of our society that 2,000 years after Christ, people are still herded together into Black ghettoes merely because their skins have different pigmentations than other people. No one condones murder or any act of violence. I hope the day shall come soon when humanity can resolve not only its racial problems but all problems coolly and rationally; when emotional acts of violence—be they individual or national—can be eliminated.

So long, however, as there exists anywhere on Earth one minority that is treated with contempt, that is herded into Black slum areas, that is abused and insulted, so long will we have violence, hate, brutality, savagery. So long as there exists a Jewish problem, or a Mexican problem—or a problem of any minority—so long will one form of violence beget another.

I am proud to be one of the humble gladiators in this struggle against narrow prejudice and stupidity. I am glad to lend my efforts so that there shall be no more James Hickman tragedies.

Frank Fried remembered that at one point she went off script, clearly moved by the audience's reaction, and said, "I love the Negro race." This brought the house down. A resolution was passed unanimously calling for James Hickman's freedom. It was an event that Fried would never forget.

At the end of the rally, it was announced that the Hickman murder trial had been postponed until November 9. Myer had requested and been granted postponement so that James Hickman could be examined by court-approved defense psychiatrists. This gave the campaign another six weeks of organizing before the start of the trial. In the previous two months the Hickman Defense Committee had organized an exciting grassroots campaign. Would another six weeks be enough to save James Hickman? Perhaps. But another horrifying tragedy would shake the city on the eve of the trial and contribute almost as much as the grassroots Hickman Defense Campaign to shaping the confrontation in the courtroom.

"It has happened, the inevitable that we feared."

10

"Holocaust" on Ohio Street

Henry Bailey, his brother-in-law, and a woman friend had been out drinking, but he decided that it was getting late and he wanted to go home. As Henry drove toward home, his brother-in-law panicked with the thought that his wife might see him with another woman. He told Henry to pull over.

They parked across the street and a little west of 940–42 West Ohio, a large four-story apartment building; in this predominantly Italian American neighborhood it was one of the few buildings occupied entirely by African Americans. It was sometime between 11:30 and 11:45 p.m. on Wednesday, October 9, 1947, a month before James Hickman was to go on trial for murder. Henry Bailey sat in the front seat of the car, and his brother-in-law and woman friend sat in the back. All three were African American.

Henry's eyes were drawn to a car parked in front of the entrance to 940–42 West Ohio. A man sat behind the steering wheel and the car's engine was running. Suddenly, two white men came running out of the building. They jumped into the waiting car, which zoomed off. He didn't get a clear look at them but thought they were between twenty-five and thirty years old with medium to thin builds. The car looked like a 1937 gray Dodge. Within twelve seconds after the Dodge pulled away, Henry turned his engine on and drove off.

William and Frances Carruthers had gone to bed early that night. The Carrutherses lived in a two-room apartment on the first floor of 942 West Ohio with their niece. Their apartment was tiny, really just one room with an adjacent kitchen. William was the janitor for the building. His daily duties included cleaning the halls and emptying the trash.

The building had been bought and "renovated" by the real estate mogul Samuel Homan two years earlier. Homan evicted the Italian American tenants, who had been paying reasonable rents, and had contractors cut up the building's twenty-two multiroom apartments into 101 rooms. He then filled the building with nearly three hundred African American tenants, whom he charged five to six times more for tiny rooms with shared bathrooms and kitchens. The Carrutherses were the first of these Black families to move into the building, on Christmas Eve 1945.

On October 9, 1947, Frances Carruthers woke up to the smell of smoke in the apartment. "I am very sensitive to smoke or gas," she later told a coroner's jury. "I choked right away at the first odor and I woke up." She sat up in bed and woke her husband.

"What is the matter?" a startled William asked her. "It must be fire," she told him. William jumped out of bed and turned on a light. He walked to the front window and saw a car driving away. The Carrutherses' apartment had two doors leading to the center hall of the building. One was in the kitchen, the other in the sleeping room with a small couch up against it.

"I raised my window. I seen a light burning in the hall, and I reached for my pants, and it was a combustion, my front window caved in on me." With this explosion, the hallway became engulfed in flames that raced to the back of the building and up the stairs. The explosion was powerful enough to blow the "bedroom door from the hinges," pushing the couch away from the door.

Fire poured into the apartment, igniting the window curtains. "All this was just in a split second," William recalled. Frances opened the kitchen door, saw that the hallway was filled with fire, and slammed the door shut.

"My God, we're trapped. We can't get out!" she screamed.

"Don't get excited," William admonished her. "We'll get out."

William grabbed a chair and broke the back kitchen window, which opened onto the alley. He helped Frances and his niece out the window and then crawled out himself. As soon as he hit the ground, he remembered the four kids in the apartment directly behind theirs. William broke the windows of that apartment and got them out. Their mother was at work. He took everyone around to the front of the building.

"The entire front entrance was burning," he remembered, "all the front of the building flaming. Fire was coming out of the third floor."

It was 12:07 a.m. when the alarm sounded at the fire station at 1125 West Chicago Avenue, about six blocks away. James F. Leahy, acting captain of the Chicago Fire Department's Fifth Battalion, jumped into his car and headed east to the fire. He was the first firefighter on the scene, and the fire's enormity hit him right away. "I got out of my car, and I told my driver to go back and sound a second alarm." Leahy saw that the whole building was threatened with destruction. "The fire was branching out, and it was obvious to me that the fire had spread to the third and fourth floors, at both sides and progressing with great rapidity."

The building had only one fire escape, and it was on the front of the 940 side. Tenants on the 942 side were cut off from it because of the fire in the hallway. Many of the 940 side tenants had to pass through one or more rooms to reach the fire escape. Locked doors prevented some from getting to it. People were gathering on the balconies of the fire escape and trying to get down. Some tenants tied sheets together and climbed out of windows to escape the flames. People were desperately trying to survive.

Leahy struggled to keep control of the situation, but it was difficult. "Panic reigned, people screaming, all the other people in the fire and about the fire screaming on all sides. The front of the building from the second floor was covered with smoke." Many more fire trucks, ladder companies, and firefighting tools were arriving on the scene. "I told the fellows the most important thing to do then was to raise the ladders to the roof, open the sky light, so that adequate ventilation [would] keep it from mushrooming."

But Leahy quickly changed his mind: rescue had to come first. "I was intently watching the operations and looking over the situation, heard a call of someone, and then to my amazement, I saw what apparently appeared to be a couple of children, three or four people at the balcony. I immediately countermanded my first order, and told the men to get the people in that landing with the main ladder."

Fire and hot, thick smoke began pouring out of the windows and stopped people from going down the fire escape. Many of the residents had just woken from a deep sleep into a living nightmare. There were many children in the building—and some of them were home alone with parents working the night shift. For Leahy this difficult situation was about to take a desperate turn. "I saw they were all panicky, everything in a more or less panicky condition, screams coming from the building."

Firefighters stretched their ladders to the fire escape balconies and held out nets below for people who might decide to jump. It was a risky way to try to save lives in the best of situations—and this wasn't the best of situations. People began to jump. Several missed the nets. Leahy saw a man and a woman lying on the sidewalk; the woman's legs were broken. He saw another child "come down through the smoke and hit the net" in the front of the building, and then another child and an older woman jumped and hit the net. He sent a team of firefighters with a net around to the back of the building. Parents fearful for their children's lives began to toss their terrified, clinging little ones into the nets below.

Willie Nunn lived with his wife and children on the fourth floor of 942. Seeing no other option, he dropped his three children, Freddie (six),

Willie James (five), and Elma (three), before he and his wife jumped. All of them survived and were taken to Cook County Hospital.

In the midst of this harrowing situation, Earl Bauer, the First Division fire marshal of the Chicago Fire Department, arrived on the scene and took command. His division covered the heart of Chicago, from the business district of the Loop near the lakefront west through the factory districts to Cicero Avenue, and south from Division Street to Twenty-Sixth Street.

"Upon my arrival there were people jumping into a net," Bauer later recalled, "[and] there had been several bodies caught in the net prior to my arrival." He ordered Leahy to get up to the third floor on the 940 side and enter the building to search for survivors. Leahy climbed a ladder with another firefighter carrying a hose to the third-floor fire escape. He stepped onto the balcony and smashed open a window. The room was an inferno, and he sprayed it with a powerful blast of water. "If we didn't have the water to cool that fire—the heat—the intensity of it, that was what we faced, and it was just sizzling in there."

Leahy crouched low to avoid the deadly smoke and fire. Soon he was crawling on his hands and knees, and suddenly, he said, "I felt my right hand come down on a victim on the floor." She was covered with soot. He wasn't sure whether she had any clothes on or whether she was alive. He picked her up and took her to another window. "I had to hurry across, I was there just in time. . . . I just didn't know where I was. I had to get out of there and open that other window and door. She was taken from me there. I never found out who she was." Leahy later found out that this woman did survive the terrifying ordeal.

Leahy and his men crossed to the 942 side of the building and found a locked door. "I kicked open that door and I walked into the room." He smashed open windows to ventilate the room, and it took a few minutes for the cloud of smoke to clear. Leahy looked under the bed, "because that is the first place you find them." Luckily, no one was there, but as he circled the room in the right-hand corner he saw, "under debris, two bodies, a woman and another body, they were tangled together."

They hadn't had a chance. The only way out for them would have been a window in an adjacent room, but the door to it was locked. The firefighters removed the bodies and sent them to the morgue.

Leahy pressed on. "I went back into the hallway, and as I got in the middle bedroom, right at that door, lying there, [there was] what appeared to be a boy or a girl, twelve or thirteen years old." He picked up the body and put it on the bed, and it was soon removed. Earl Bauer entered the building on the first floor and worked his way up the stairs with several firefighters and a fire hose. "I got to the balcony of the third floor in between the sections there of 940 and 942. I found the body of an infant baby on the balcony, close to the window." In the rear bedroom, Bauer found four more bodies.

Among the dead discovered by Leahy and Bauer were six members of the Griggs-Hector-Williams family: Bessie Hector (age thirty-seven), Almarita Hector (two), Ruth Griggs (twenty-nine), Lena Jean Griggs (twelve), Joseph Griggs Jr. (three), and John Lewis Griggs (one). They lived in the rear of the third floor of 942. Willie Mae Williams, the eldest sister of Bessie and Ruth, was working the night of the fire. She was the breadwinner in the family, working two jobs while her two sisters raised the children. They had been among the first Black tenants in the building.

"I am out working all the time," Willie Mae later testified. "I have lived in this building very little, working all the time, and under conditions you need four jobs if you want to get some place. I'd have four if the good Lord would give me any more strength, but he just gives me strength to hold the two." She worked twelve hours a day and took home barely two hundred dollars a month after taxes. Willie Mae was contacted at work and told of the tragedy and asked to come to the morgue to identify the bodies.

Rosie McAllister was working at her job in a shoe factory the night of the fire. Her two sisters, Mary (thirty-three) and Bertha (fourteen), died in the fire in the fourth-floor rear apartment; a friend who was staying with them, Bertha McDowell, jumped to safety and was taken to Cook County Hospital.

Angeline McDonald lived on the fourth floor of 942 with her ten-year-old daughter, Jessie. The night of the fire Angeline was at work at the Container Corporation of America. Jessie was alone when she woke up; she put on her coat to escape the flames but collapsed and died before she could get out. She was found in the middle room that she shared with her mother.

Jack Smith was an unemployed janitor. He lived on the third floor of 940 West Ohio with his pregnant wife, Drusilla, and their small child. Drusilla shook Jack awake and told him something was wrong. He opened the door of their apartment and saw the stairwell on fire. He closed the door, grabbed their child, and made his way through several rooms and out a window onto the fire escape. In the confusion of the moment he lost track of Drusilla. "I thought she was behind me but she was not," Smith later told the coroner's jury. He identified his wife's body at the morgue.

Firefighters would keep the hoses trained on the building for several more hours until the last dying embers were cold. A large number of apartments were completely destroyed by the fire, and many others were water damaged. On his way out, Leahy went into the Carrutherses' apartment. He looked around the room and noticed that their clock was charred and had stopped at 12:07 a.m.

Hundreds of neighborhood residents had gathered around the ruined building: the besieged and devastated Black residents huddled on one corner, while a larger white crowd had assembled on another. No one from the crowd of whites extended a helping hand to their Black neighbors who had been driven into the cool autumn night with only the clothes on their backs. Reporters and photographers from all of Chicago's daily newspapers milled about on Ohio Street, which was crammed with an array of fire trucks, ambulances, patrol wagons, and police cars. A *Chicago Tribune* photographer snapped a picture of Police Inspector E. J. Daly, city attorney Earl Downes, and policeman Chester Daniels examining a coffee can found in the stairwell of the fire-wracked building. A *Chicago Daily News* reporter asked Leahy if the fire was arson or an accident.

"No fire," Leahy told him, "could get such a head without an artificial stimulation." The dead were taken by ambulance or patrol wagon to the morgue for identification and examination. Ten badly burned bodies were laid out on the floor of the morgue.

The survivors had been left homeless and needed shelter, food, and clothing. The Red Cross quickly came to the scene, but the bulk of support work would be done by the staff of the Chicago Commons, a community center on Grand Avenue, a block from the fire.

Chicago Commons was modeled on the more famous Hull House. Lea Demarest Taylor was its director. Her father, Graham Taylor, had established Chicago Commons in the fall of 1894. Taylor was on the faculty of the Chicago Theological Seminary, where he taught applied Christianity. Wanting to live in a working-class immigrant community, he chose an Irish, German, and Scandinavian neighborhood just north and west of the Loop that over the next two decades transitioned into being mostly Italian. Taylor started a kindergarten, clubs, and English classes.

In 1901, Chicago Commons expanded and constructed a five-story building on Grand Avenue with a gymnasium, auditorium, activities rooms, and living quarters for about two dozen residents. Lea Demarest Taylor succeeded her father as director in 1922 and remained in the post for the next three decades. As small numbers of African Americans began to move to the Northwest Side in the 1940s, she created programs to meet their needs at Chicago Commons. Lea Taylor witnessed firsthand the longtime Italian American residents' growing hostility toward their new Black neighbors. She knew of the terrible conditions that her Black clients endured and of the real estate practices of slumlords like Sam Homan. She tried to promote racial harmony and goodwill by sponsoring interracial dances, camping outings, and other events, but to no avail.

The painful events of October 10, 1947, represented the culmination of all her fears. "It has happened, the inevitable that we feared," she wrote to friends the afternoon following the fire. "The people leaping down out of the flames will not soon be forgotten, nor the mother for whom we had to send at the industry in which she worked nights, in order to take her to the morgue where her only child—a little girl of twelve lay dead." For Taylor the events of that night were "the worst disaster in the field of inter-racial warfare that has happened in Chicago." Many of those who died in the fire or were injured were well known to the staff at Chicago Commons.

Lea and her staff struggled to cope with the disaster. "We opened the house immediately and served coffee to all. Sixty people slept in the auditorium and woman's club room, the neighborhood parlor and lobby—a silent, pathetic, quiet and stunned group," wrote Taylor . "The staff were grand and were up most of the night and have worked all day at the regular things. We have to house some people tonight, and probably over the weekend, but I hope space can be found for them somewhere."

Finding new homes for the survivors would be a struggle. "Some of them are able to return to their flats today, as only one double entry way of the large building burned, but sixteen families are completely burned out, and quite a number of them in the hospital seriously injured."

Taylor went to Cook County Hospital and the morgue and made a detailed report listing the dead, the injured, what apartments and floors they lived in, the size of the families, whether they jumped or were thrown to safety, and in some cases how much they paid for rent. Sixty people in all, one in five who lived in the building, had been injured and taken to Cook County Hospital for medical treatment.

The following morning a weary and exhausted Lea Taylor led a small delegation to city hall to meet with Mayor Martin Kennelly.

The son of a packinghouse worker, Kennelly had used his experience as a quartermaster during the First World War to develop a thriving moving and storage business, Allied Van Lines. A lifelong bachelor, Kennelly lived on the far northern end of Lake Shore Drive at the luxurious Edgewater Beach Hotel. Its pink buildings were a favorite destination for presidents and other celebrities visiting Chicago.

The Democratic machine had nominated Kennelly to save itself after the notoriously corrupt regime of the previous three-term Democratic mayor, Edward J. Kelly. Winning on April Fool's Day 1947 by a record margin of 273,000 votes over his Republican opponent, Kennelly benefited in part from a racist backlash at timid and extremely limited efforts at integrating public housing under Mayor Kelly.

Lea Taylor, Tom Wright of the Mayor's Commission, and Thomas Underwood, board president of Chicago Commons, met with Mayor Kennelly at 9:00 a.m. at his office. He claimed not to know about the Ohio Street disaster, according to Taylor, but he "promised all possible help in ferreting out the trouble." "We asked for a 'blue ribbon' jury—prominent people," said Taylor, "and he promised it for the [coroner's] inquest."

By this time, whether Kennelly was aware of it or not, the Ohio Street fire was front-page news, and as the horrific events of the night became widely known, it was creating a political crisis for city hall. The *Chicago Tribune*'s headlines were "10 Killed in Tenement Fire" and "14 Hurt in W. Ohio Street. Flats; Suspect Arson." The 940–42 West Ohio building wasn't at the far reaches of the city; it was a little over a mile from city hall. William Touhy, the state's attorney for Cook County, and Captain George Homer of the Racine Avenue police station visited the burned-out tenement. The coroner's inquest into the deaths on Ohio Street would have to be handled differently. The coroner's jury would have to be made up of credible, respectable people, not unknowns, including leaders from the Black community.

Political power in Cook County was concentrated in one building in Chicago's Loop. The monumental Chicago City Hall and Cook County Building takes up an entire city block. The west side of the building housed the offices of the mayor, city treasurer, and aldermen, while the east side of the building housed the county offices, including the coroner's office. Mayor Kennelly's office was only a short walk from Coroner Brodie's office. During the two days that followed the fire, a search took place to identify the people who would make up the "blue-ribbon" jury that Lea Taylor and others demanded.

Soon after Taylor left Kennelly's office, a delegation from the Hickman Defense Committee arrived. Willoughby Abner, Sid Lens, and Henry McGee met with Kennelly and demanded that in the wake of the carnage and death on Ohio Street, Kennelly put before the city council an amendment to the city fire ordinance that would place landlords who violated the ordinance in jail rather than be let off with small fines. They pointed out that there had been 751 fires from November 1946 through the end of January 1947, in which fourteen people had died. The fire at 1733 West Washburne Street had led to the shooting of the landlord. They pressed Mayor Kennelly further: they requested that he order an immediate inspection of any unsafe building and that the fire code be rigidly enforced.

He asked the group for specific examples of violations of the fire code. They gave several examples, and he promised to act on one of them immediately. But he made no promises about changing the city ordinances. The delegation left and issued a press release about the meeting with Kennelly on CIO Industrial Union Council letterhead.

Sensing that something was up after these meetings with Taylor's and Abner's delegations, Kennelly paid a short visit to 940–42 West Ohio Street around noon. Pressure to act was also coming from the editorial pages of Marshall Field's *Chicago Sun*. "Was the Fire Set?" headlined the *Sun*'s editorial on Saturday. "It is hard to believe that anybody should be so heartless as to set a fire that jeopardized the lives of 300 persons, and actually killed ten. The entire resources of the city's investigation machinery should be thrown into discovering the truth about this tragedy."

By Saturday morning, the morning of the inquest, Brodie had found six men, three Black and three white, to serve on the jury. He had asked Horace Cayton, a sociologist who directed the Parkway Community House on the city's South Side, to be the jury foreman, and Cayton had agreed. Horace Cayton was a large man with short, slicked-back hair and a high forehead. A thin beard that ran along his jawline outlined his wide face. His dark eyes could reveal a hidden sadness or a sharp intelligence, depending on his mood. He always dressed well and carried himself with a sense of confidence. The choice of Cayton was good for the Hickman Defense Committee; the Parkway Community Center had hosted some of its meetings.

Brodie asked Cayton to raise his right had and take the oath of office:

> You, as foreman to this inquest, do solemnly swear, that you will diligently
> inquire, and true presentment make, how, and in what manner, and by
> whom or what the body which here lies dead, came to its death; and that
> you will deliver to me, the coroner of the county, a true inquest thereof,
> according to such evidence as shall be given to you, and according to the
> best of your knowledge and belief; so help you, God.

Cayton took the oath. The rest of the jury included Dr. Arthur Falls,
a well-known physician in the Black community; Patrick O'Reilly, an
insurance broker and a leading figure in the City Club; Leo Lonigan,
vice president of McKesson and Robbins; Sidney Williams of the Urban
League; and Earl McMahon, secretary-treasurer of the AFL's Chicago
Building Trades Council.

"The fire appears to be of incendiary origin," Brodie told the jurors
in his opening remarks. "Maybe it was not, but the suspicion still is there.
I want you to ferret out the cause. Please spare nobody. If it was caused
by carelessness of any city inspector or anybody else, I want it brought
out at the inquest. You have a complete right of investigation."

The coroner's noble intentions would soon be called into question
as the inquest became a contest of wills between Brodie, who wanted to
keep a small lens focused on the Ohio Street fire, and Cayton, who
wanted a wider-ranging investigation.

Horace Cayton had been battling depression for two years. His doctor
warned him "to avoid tense situations, especially those involving race."
But he was enraged after reading newspaper stories about the Ohio Street
fire. "Ten Negroes had escaped the South only to be burned on an altar
of neglect, indifference, greed, and racial bias," he later recalled. For the
next two days the senseless deaths on Ohio Street hung heavily on his
mind. He was "jarred" from his depression by Brodie's request that he
serve as jury foreman. At first he hesitated—he was truly worried about

his mental health. But he couldn't say no. "The coroner insisted, and I was not unaware of the importance of the case in view of the changing racial patterns throughout the city."

That was an understatement. Horace Cayton was the coauthor, along with St. Clair Drake, of *Black Metropolis*, a pioneering study of Black life in Chicago in the 1930s and early 1940s. Published in 1945, it was greeted as a literary event in liberal and progressive circles in the North. Richard Wright wrote the introduction and called it "a landmark of research and scientific achievement." Cayton and Drake devoted an entire chapter to the evolution of the Black Belt in Chicago. They were well versed in the various practices and tricks used by real estate interests, landlords, and large "respectable" institutions like the University of Chicago to isolate and prey upon the city's South Side Black population.

Born in 1901 in Seattle, Washington, Horace Cayton came from an extraordinary family. His grandfather Hiram R. Revels had been the first African American elected to the US Senate during Reconstruction. His father, Horace R. Cayton Sr., was a newspaper publisher in Seattle, where few Blacks lived at the turn of the twentieth century; he and his wife Susan, Hiram Revels's daughter, had three children. Horace's younger brother Revels Cayton joined the Communist Party and became a prominent member of the Marine Cooks and Stewards Union in San Francisco during the 1934 general strike, and a leading figure in the California labor movement.

Cayton first came to Chicago in the fall of 1931, seeking a fellowship at the University of Chicago. "Never had I seen so many Negroes; it came almost as a shock to see so many dark faces. In Seattle I had seen perhaps a hundred or more together at some special affair, but I was unprepared for this sea of black, olive, and brown faces everywhere."

On his first day in Chicago, while eating at a small restaurant, he looked up and saw a large crowd of Blacks marching down the street. Curious, he quickly got up and joined the march. It was one of the many marches organized by the Communist Party's Unemployed

Councils to stop the eviction of unemployed families from their homes. Soon after the marchers arrived at a designated address, a Black woman started to address the crowd, but then suddenly a mob of Chicago police attacked it.

"I had never seen hungry people before," Cayton explained later. "Cruelty and brutality I had experienced, but never anything like what I came to know in the early days of the Depression in Chicago."

During the next decade Cayton rose to prominence as a scholar and researcher, traveling and teaching in other cities. "By the time the United States had entered World War II, I had become what Negroes call a 'race leader' and a 'race man.'" Despite the pressure of wartime unity and patriotism, he wasn't afraid to take principled positions. In 1942, he wrote an article for the *Nation* called "Fighting for White Folks" that "caused me much trouble, and I was immediately called up by my draft board." He was opposed to "fight[ing] in a Jim Crow army." The military reclassified him 1-A, and he faced the possibility of being immediately drafted in the army. He was relieved when the military announced that it would cease drafting men over thirty-eight.

On Monday morning October 13, Chicago awoke to a front-page offer by Marshall Field III in the *Chicago Sun*. In bold black letters was the headline "$1,000 Reward." The caption read: "The Chicago Sun will pay a reward of $1,000 for evidence leading to the arrest and conviction of any person or persons criminally responsible for the deaths of the 10 victims in the fire at 940–42 Ohio St., last Thursday night." The Negro Chamber of Commerce added another thousand dollars to the reward and was soon joined by the *Chicago Defender* and the Chicago Civil Liberties Committee, each contributing five hundred. The reward now came to three thousand dollars, the equivalent of thirty thousand today.

The *Daily News* ran a large photo of the coroner's jury and A. L. Brodie making an on-site investigation of the 940–42 West Ohio building over the weekend. The interracial jury was seen examining the charred, debris-filled ruins of one part of the building. The accompanying article, "Tenement Conditions Appall Fire Probers," quoted Horace Cayton: "We're going to get down to the bottom of the mess. We're not only interested in the immediate cause of the fire, but also the reason for the existence of such living conditions." The inspection created a small commotion in the neighborhood as reporters, police, and firemen accompanied them.

A young Black woman, Ernestine Lyles, asked Cayton to look at the three-room apartment that she and her husband occupied with six other people. Ernestine and her husband paid thirty-six dollars a month for their share of the space. The overcrowding was suffocating and dangerous. Brodie, Cayton, and the rest of the jury also met with Lea Taylor at the nearby Chicago Commons settlement so that she could go over the living conditions in the neighborhood with them. When Cayton learned from her that Sam Homan owned other properties in the area, he wanted the jury to immediately inspect them to see whether the dangerous conditions that led to ten deaths on Ohio Street also existed in these properties. Homan didn't disappoint. Brodie and the jury drove to a tenement a little more than a mile away and found that it had no fire escapes and no rear exits. After speaking to the residents, they discovered that the building had twenty-one rooms occupied by sixty-five people.

Walking amid the debris in the 940–42 West Ohio building and going floor to floor peering into the charred living quarters made Cayton even more determined to establish the immediate cause of the fire and expose "before the public the whole background of city neglect, the way in which Negroes were forced to live under such scandalous conditions by unscrupulous real estate dealers, and the general corruption of the city government." He and the other two Black jurors, Sidney Williams and Arthur Falls, would form a bloc to keep the pressure on Brodie.

Brodie was a prominent figure in Chicago politics, and Cayton was well aware of city hall's influence on him, but he had seen him only from a distance. As the jury foreman, Cayton had an opportunity to take the measure of the man up close. "The coroner was politically ambitious and by dramatizing the case hoped to win votes among Negroes. But he had not counted on the vigor with which we Negro jurors would attack the case," he recalled fifteen years later in his autobiography, *Long Old Road*.

The inquest into the ten deaths on Ohio Street would involve five public hearings, only two of which would take place before the murder trial of James Hickman, but the horrendous conditions, neglect by public authorities, and personal stories of tragic loss would be disseminated throughout the city by Chicago's five daily newspapers and the weekly *Chicago Defender*. If there was a time during the fire crisis of 1947 when the issues that drove James Hickman to shoot and kill David Coleman were the clearest to the broad public, it was the three weeks leading up to his trial.

When Brodie called to order the "Inquest Upon the Bodies of Ruth Griggs, et al" on Tuesday, October 14, 1947, at 10:00 a.m. at the county morgue, the room was tense with anticipation. It had been five days since the fire, and the newspapers reports and the jury's on-site investigations produced an overflow crowd in the small hearing room. Packed with surviving tenants and relatives, firefighters, and cops, it was standing room only. A large diagram of 940–42 West Ohio Street hung on the wall showing floors, rooms, and where each deceased was found. A besieged Samuel Homan, surrounded by his lawyer and staff from his real estate company, sat near the front of the room at a long wooden table. Knowing that Homan had been subpoenaed to be at the inquest, tenant rights activists from his buildings across the city had come to confront him and list for the jury the problems they had dealing with him. Representing the State's Attorney's Office was Assistant State's Attorney Blair Varnes. The Chicago Fire Department and Police Department were respectively represented by Fire Marshal Earl Bauer and Captain George Homer, whose Racine Avenue district included the site of the Ohio Street fire. Earl Downes, the assistant corporation counsel, represented the City of Chicago.

"Let the record show," Brodie told those assembled, "that the jury has been duly qualified and sworn over the bodies of the herein named deceased person." He asked them one last time whether any of them could not render a fair and impartial verdict or for any other reason could not serve. All of them replied that they could serve. "The jury stands accepted," declared Brodie.

"At first, the coroner and the police treated us with great courtesy and respect," Cayton recalled of the first two days of hearings. But tension began to build between them from the examination of the very first witness.

Willie Mae Williams had lost six members of her family in the fire, and she testified about the terrible conditions in which she and her family lived. She told the jury that in June 1946, when her mother was visiting from St. Louis, she had heard threats from hostile white neighbors. "Honey, be careful, there is trouble brewing, we are going to be burned out," her mother warned.

When Cayton asked her how much income she earned and what proportion of that went for rent, Brodie chastised him. "Let's not go into that and make an issue as such." An annoyed Cayton barked back at him: "May I finish questioning the witness?" Brodie replied, "Surely, Mr. Cayton."

A few minutes later Brodie turned his ire toward Willie Mae Williams, telling her to stop "cluttering up the record," when she tried to give clear answers to Cayton's questions. Brodie was on the hot seat, squeezed between city hall and Cayton, the jury, and relatives of the deceased who wanted to get the truth behind the fire.

On October 15, the second day of hearings, things finally came to a head between Brodie and Cayton. During a break, Cayton revealed to Brodie that he had taken some debris from the fire and had it tested at the University of Chicago. He didn't trust the police crime lab. The tests had proved conclusively that arson was the cause of the fire. Brodie, "trembling with anger" according to Cayton, called him and police and fire officials into his office. He wanted to give Cayton a dressing down. "Goddamn it, Cayton, you're not running Cook County!" Brodie screamed. Captain Homer warned Cayton that the West Side was ready to explode in a riot. Cayton replied that the only way to prevent violence was for "the truth to come out, with all the evidence."

Brodie saw that the whole situation was slipping out of his control. "You're going too far, Cayton." Captain Homer asked, "What exactly do you want, Mr. Cayton?" Cayton told Homer that he wanted the police department to publicly admit that this was an arson case, and that he wanted the criminals caught. He was sure the police already had a good idea who the killers were, but were not being forthright.

Brodie began to calm down, though he undoubtedly realized that his political future might be on the line. He asked Cayton how thoroughly he intended to investigate the case. Cayton told him he would do whatever needed to be done to get at the truth.

A bewildered Brodie asked him, "What do you mean by that?"

Cayton replied: "I intend to subpoena the head of the building department and ask him when the house was last inspected and why it was passed. Some of the people who were burned to death would have had to go through two or three other apartments to get to a fire escape. This violates a number of city building codes, so I want to know who approved the conversion of the building. Then I want to question the owner about his exorbitant rents. I also intend to subpoena other real estate dealers who are making a fortune charging Negro families forty-five dollars or more a month to rent one room. That's as far as I've got, but there may be more."

"All right, Mr. Cayton, you've made your point," Captain Homer said with a cool anger in his voice. "I'll assign Lieutenant Dooley and six men to report directly to you on the investigation. As to the rest, Brodie, that's up to you. Next time you pick a blue-ribbon jury, choose more carefully."

The explosive testimony at the first two hearings was highlighted in the afternoon editions of the daily press. The *Chicago Daily News* headline on Wednesday, October 15, blared, "Tests Point to Arson in Tenement Fire," while the *Sun* ran a summary of the day's testimony under the headline "Death Trap Owner Ignores Hazards, Witnesses Say." The third hearing would not be held until November 1 to give the various city departments time to collect the material that Cayton wanted brought before the jury. Meanwhile, the Black community mourned and buried its dead.

"The full impact of the firetrap tenement was brought tragically to the attention of an estimated 10,000 persons who viewed the charred remains of six unfortunate victims of the disastrous fire at 940–42 Ohio Street," reported the *Chicago Defender*. The wakes and funerals of the victims were outpourings of grief. The O. F. Douglas Funeral Home was crowded all day long on Sunday as a steady stream of friends, relatives, community leaders, and those who had read or heard about the tragedy came to express their sympathy for the victims' families.

When reporters at the *Chicago Defender* got the opportunity to vent their rage, they didn't mince words. Vernon Jarrett called the mass deaths "a holocaust" and pointed the finger of guilt at the "blood-stained hands of restrictive covenants." For Jarrett the laws on the books worked hand in hand with the white mob violence that forced "Negroes [to] live in fire traps such as the charred near Northside apartment building."

"Words, Words, Words," howled a piece by another *Chicago Defender* reporter, Louise Stephens, "against fire hazards which hundreds spoke in the city's schools, theaters, churches, and clubs became a mockery." The editor chose an appropriately ironic title for her article: "Slum Blaze Climaxes Fire Prevention Week." Stephens believed things could get worse in the coming winter. "The city had its first warning of what lay in store for its citizens unless prompt and effective measures are taken to halt the 1947 death toll." The mounting toll of fire deaths had placed what she called "an X marks the death spot" for Chicago with "a persistent series of fire and a mounting death toll. Children died. Their parents died. Hundreds were made homeless. The death toll from the winter fires in Bronzeville alone was 22. For the city it was well over 100."

Racial covenants, arson, mob violence, landlord greed, and the indifference and corruption of the city and county authorities created cascading crises for Chicago's Black community. "This year housing conditions are, if possible, worse than before," warned Stephens. "In July alone more than 200 families were evicted from their homes and, presumably, most of them must have found shelter in the homes of other people, relatives and friends. This is the explanation for 10 people or 15 people to a room in many areas of the city."

The following day the funeral for the Griggs-Hector-Williams family was held at the St. Paul Church of God in Christ. Reverend Louis Henry Ford was the church's pastor. He had come to Chicago from Mississippi as a teenager with twenty-five cents in his pocket in 1933, during the depths of the Depression. A sharecropper's son, he preached on street corners until he build his church into one of the largest on the South Side.

The six white-draped coffins were displayed at the front of the church. The surviving relatives were so poor that the services of the morticians, churches, and livery companies were donated or had been covered by the Defender Charities or the Red Cross. The funeral service began at one o'clock in the afternoon, with over five thousand angry, restless people crammed into Reverend Ford's church. Police were stationed throughout the church to keep order, while an overflow crowd gathered outside. The St. Paul Choir and trio, the soloist Curtis Nelson, and the Campbell Harmoneers sang at the services. The most emotional hymn was "I'll Fly Away," written in 1929 by Alfred E. Brumley, a favorite in Baptist and Church of God churches. Brumley had spent much of his youth chopping cotton on his family's farm in Oklahoma.

When the shadows of this life have gone,
I'll fly away;
Like a bird from prison bars has flown,
I'll fly away.
Just a few more weary days and then,
I'll fly away;
To a land where joy shall never end,
I'll fly away.

Three-minute remarks were given by Alderman William Harvey and John M. Ragland of the South Central Association. Blaming the deaths on restrictive covenants, Henry McGee of the NAACP called on the mourners to join the NAACP and other organizations to "fight those working against us." David M. Kellum (Bud Billiken), who had spent much of the previous year organizing a fire awareness campaign, told those assembled, "Their deaths should serve as a warning to those of us who are forced to live in firetraps similar to those in which they died." Horace Cayton declared, "The cause of this fire will be found, and conditions under which people are forced to live like these will be exposed." Reverend Ford gave the closing sermon and presented the surviving family members with a one-hundred-dollar donation from his congregation. After the service, the pastors, family, and friends made the long drive to the suburb of Burr Oak, where they laid the victims of the fire to rest.

The work of finding the cause of the fire and the killers had just begun for Cayton and the rest of the coroner's jury, and it would be a hard slog. Years later Cayton wearily recalled "weeks of struggle with reluctant witnesses, hostile police, and the frightened but still uncooperative coroner. The head of the building department testified that the house had last been inspected two years previous to the fire, but that the man who had passed it was no longer working for the city and could not be located. The police reported that they had an arson suspect but later claimed that he had eluded them. Even my liberal white friends, who had at first encouraged me, became alarmed at some of the disclosures before the jury." Two white witnesses, whom the press had initially hailed as heroes for saving lives during the fire, gave such contradictory and convoluted testimony about why they were at the fire that many came to believe that they might have had direct knowledge of the cause of the fire and who had set it.

After five public hearings and over one thousand pages of testimony taken, the jury deliberated and came to a unanimous verdict that Cayton was put in charge of writing. It was delivered to the coroner on the morning of December 12, 1947, and read into the record. The thirty-page verdict was an indictment of the entire power structure of Chicago and its practices, and it included clear recommendations to the state's attorney and pleas for justice:

> We, the Jury, find the cause of the fire, in which the four women and six children named above, lost their lives in the early morning of October 10, to be of an incendiary [nature].
>
> We do not find, at this time, sufficient evidence to charge any individual or individuals with the crime. We do, however, charge that the person or

persons unknown with *murder by arson*. It is our conviction that such a callous crime must *not* go unpunished. The murderer or murderers are at large.

The jury called upon the police to continue their investigations and the state's attorney "to use every means at his disposal to bring the murderer or murderers to justice." The statement continued:

> We, the Jury, find the unbelievably shocking conditions in the death building at 940–42 West Ohio Street—the overcrowding, the vicious violations of safety and building code provisions and of ordinary standards of decency—to be directly contributory to the deaths of ten trapped women and children.
>
> *The Jury cannot stress too strongly its belief that there would have been no deaths in this tenement had the operator had even the slightest feelings of human decency toward his tenants.*
>
> We therefore request that the State's Attorney begin an immediate and detailed investigation of the conditions of the building and all similar multiple dwellings with which Samuel Homan, a real estate operator, is in any way connected.
>
> We recommend, further, that the State's Attorney determine whether Samuel Homan can be held on a charge of *criminal negligence*.

The jurors were "appalled at the inefficiency and laxity of Chicago's building practices: practices which in our opinion, suffer violations of safety regulations, of building code provisions, of ordinary standards of human decency to exist unchecked year after year."

Finally, the jury concluded that the Ohio Street fire reflected a disturbing pattern:

> This tragedy, far from being an isolated incident, is rather a symptom of a pattern of social ills festering throughout the city.
>
> We were shocked that the fire which flared so tragically on West Ohio Street, sweeping with it the lives of ten innocent and unsuspecting human beings, has its counterpart—actual or potential—in many Chicago neighborhoods.

The responsibility for these terrible conditions lay "at the doorstep of the Police Department, the Building Inspection Department, real estate operators and boards, and thousands of home owners throughout Chicago." The Ohio Street fire was one case exemplifying many others. "It highlights dramatically the long established practice which enriches unscrupulous landlords in Chicago—landlords who place money above human lives."

After the verdict was read, Horace Cayton left the coroner's office and went home. Failing to heed his doctor's warnings to avoid stressful situations, he had selflessly thrown himself into securing justice for ten people he didn't know, and it had taken its toll on him. Not only was he exhausted from weeks of hearings, but he couldn't get out his head the image of the ten charred bodies he had seen lying on the floor of the county morgue. "I returned to my apartment and tried to sleep. I found myself pacing the floor in uncontrollable rage and frustration." His rage turned to despair. "It was a hopeless situation, and all the efforts I had expended would be forgotten in a few weeks, when in all probability another fire would kill more defenseless black people." Finally he called his secretary and told her to call his doctor—he was sure he was having a nervous breakdown.

Horace Cayton spent the better part of the next decade in and out of mental health institutions. No one was ever prosecuted for the ten murders on Ohio Street.

"This was God fixed this. I had raised these children up and God knowed the vow I made to him ... that these children was a generation to be raised up. God wasn't pleased what happened to them."

11

"This man has paid enough"

After Samuel Freeman had announced that the prosecution would try James Hickman for murder, Mike Myer was in need of a collaborating attorney whose judgment he could trust, someone who was not afraid of controversy and, most importantly, could work closely with the Hickman Defense Committee. Myer didn't have to think about it very long; in fact, one person came to mind right away. Mike Myer's and Leon Despres's law offices were both located in the Chicago Temple building, the beehive of attorneys near city hall. Myer walked down the hall and knocked on Despres's door.

Born Leon Mathis Despres in 1908, he was son of Samuel Despres, a businessman active in civic affairs. Leon was raised in a comfortable middle-class home in the Hyde Park neighborhood of Chicago. When Despres was a kid, exploring his neighborhood was an adventure. Hyde Park still had a nineteenth-century feel. He later recalled that when he walked into his backyard, the wide alleyways always held a parade of colorful characters. Junkmen called out for rags and old iron. For a few coins, musicians would sing anything from Irish ballads to Italian arias. There were men playing the hurdy-gurdy (a fiddle played by turning a hand-cranked rosined wheel against the strings), and an organ grinder with a monkey on his shoulder would crank out tunes. The monkey would tip his cap, urging the gathered crowd of listeners to make a donation in appreciation. Horse-drawn wagons piled high with merchandise moved up and down the streets, while workmen plied their trade and fruit and vegetable peddlers filled the morning air with loud pitches for their produce. Ninety years later, Despres told his biographer that the mornings in Hyde Park were "very much like the opening scene of the French opera *Louise*." It was a great time and place to be a kid.

Just three years younger than Myer, Despres grew up in a Chicago where Clarence Darrow, Jane Addams, and Eugene Debs were major figures. It was a city of overworked, underpaid factory workers, ruthless employers, and corrupt politicians, but it was also a place where progressive, socialist, communist, and feminist ideas were as freely available as the booze that flowed during Prohibition.

After his father died, Despres's mother sent him to study for two years of high school in Italy and France, and he learned to speak both French and Italian. After completing high school, he went to the University of Chicago in his old neighborhood, where he received his undergraduate and law degrees in 1927 and 1929, on the eve of the Depression. Like many novice attorneys, he was hired by a large law firm and given assignments that involved the foreclosure of delinquent home mortgages. Despres, who was already something of a socialist, hated the work. He soon quit and started his own law firm. In 1931 he married Marian Alschuler, daughter of renowned Chicago architect Alfred S. Alschuler.

Despres joined the Socialist Party in 1933. He was drawn to the Trotskyist "Appeal" caucus in the party and became close friends with Albert Goldman, Mike Myer, and another left-wing labor and civil rights lawyer, Francis Heisler. He left the Socialist Party after the Trotskyists were expelled in 1937, but he did not join the newly formed Socialist Workers Party.

Early in his legal career Despres began representing unions in their disputes with employers. He always believed it a privilege to do so. "To act in the workers' behalf has been wonderful, exciting my mind, my blood, and my heart." The work didn't pay very well. Cash-strapped local unions had very little money for lawyers—unlike the bosses, who hired the biggest legal firms in the city. "I was lucky sometimes to get five dollars an hour, and sometimes I got nothing," Despres recalled. In one union drive at a candy factory, his language skills were unexpectedly needed. The CIO wanted to organize the thousands of workers employed in candy factories in the greater Chicago area. "In one plant all the workers were Italian. Since I had gone to high school in Italy, I was asked to address the employees in Italian and tell them that what the superintendent was doing was not in their best interests. They listened, and they ended up supporting the union."

The victory at the candy factory was sweet, but Chicago was a steel town, and the future of the industrial union movement rested on what happened in the big steel mills on the South Side. The CIO suffered one of its worst setbacks over Memorial Day weekend, 1937. U.S. Steel, the largest steel producer in the country, had signed a contract with the CIO's Steel Workers Organizing Committee (SWOC) on March 17. Myron Taylor, chairman of U.S. Steel, wanted to avoid the costly sit-down strikes that had shut down General Motors during the previous winter. But Taylor's five major competitors, Bethlehem Steel, Youngstown Sheet and Tube, Republic Steel, and Inland Steel, collectively known as "Little Steel," were not interested in an agreement. They began to stockpile weapons and ammunition for the coming battle with the union. On May 26, 1937, the SWOC called a national strike against Little Steel for union recognition, and seventy-five thousand workers went out on strike across the country. The strike was as close to being 100 percent effective as one could have hoped for. It also coincided with the Memorial Day weekend, a time of picnics and other outdoor festivities.

The CIO was counting on the support of its New Deal allies, like Chicago's Mayor Ed Kelly and the governors of the key states of Illinois,

Ohio, and Pennsylvania, where the strike had its biggest impact. This proved to be a serious miscalculation, as the governors and mayors of these states mobilized the local and state police and the National Guard against the strikers.

The SWOC called a rally for Memorial Day, May 30, on the South Side of Chicago near the Republic Steel mill. Mayor Kelly sent hundreds of police, at the request of Republic Steel, to keep the plant open. He then promptly left town, leaving Captain Mooney in charge of the police detail. Believing that they had a right to peaceful picketing guaranteed by the recent Supreme Court decision to uphold the Wagner Act, about fifteen hundred people, including the wives and children of strikers, marched across an open field toward the Republic Steel mill.

The marchers were in a festive mood as they crossed the trash-strewn field. It was an unseasonably warm day—the temperature had climbed to nearly 90 degrees. The police were lined up in front of the plant, nearly two hundred of them, wearing their winter uniforms, their badges glittering in the bright sunlight. An advance group of marchers were talking to the police when suddenly a blue haze of uniforms rushed across the field, clubbing and shooting at the unarmed striking workers and their families. More than one hundred people were beaten, fifty were shot, and ten died from gunshot wounds. Many of those murdered that day by Chicago police were shot in the back.

Despres was playing tennis at his in-laws' home in the wealthy North Shore suburb of Winnetka when he was called by a doctor working at the union's clinic. He rushed back to the city. He had been a member of the Lawyers Constitutional Rights Committee, which supported the workers trying to organize at Little Steel. Despres played a significant role in the aftermath of the Memorial Day massacre. The antiunion and viciously anticommunist *Chicago Daily Tribune* attempted to create a virtual vigilante atmosphere in the city in an effort to crush the CIO. One *Tribune* editorial—"Murder in South Chicago"—claimed that the peaceful marchers were trying to storm the Republic Steel mill; it called them a "murderous mob . . . inflamed by speeches of CIO organizers." In the minds of the *Tribune* editorial writers, civilization itself was at stake. The heroic Chicago police had prevented "anarchy." It was time for the state's attorney and the courts to move into action. "It remains for the other law enforcement officers of the community to finish the job in the criminal courts," the *Tribune* advised.

While the *Tribune* called for the CIO leaders' heads, fury roiled through Chicago's working-class neighborhoods, while radicals, liberals, and progressives, anyone with a scintilla of social consciousness, joined the chorus of outrage. Despres helped organize a citizens' committee that investigated the role of the police in the massacre. It held a rally at the cavernous art deco–style Civic Opera House to protest the massacre and demand a full investigation that would hold those responsible for it accountable for their actions. More than thirty-five hundred turned out for this rally, a week after Memorial Day.

"Workers should have the right to organize," Despres told the crowd. A young Studs Terkel was in the audience that night and later remembered that Despres "spoke from the heart." The poet and Lincoln biographer Carl Sandburg was also on the stage that night; he read a very angry and eloquent speech with the reoccurring line "The score was ten to nothing."

Many of the city's best-known liberals, such as University of Chicago professor Paul Douglas, a future US senator, and Robert Morss Lovett, associate editor of the *New Republic*, took the stage to denounce the Chicago police. The nearly seventy-year-old Lovett cried out, "Captain Mooney is a killer!"

The Memorial Day massacre deepened Leon Despres's commitment to the labor movement. He had helped railroad baggage handlers or porters, popularly known as Red Caps, to organize a union. A Chicago Red Cap, Willard Saxby Townsend, had begun organizing the railroad porters in 1934 and fought for them to gain employee status with the railroads. Until 1938 they earned only tips. The porters formed the International Brotherhood of Red Caps (IBRC) in 1937, and a few years later they changed their name to the United Transport Service Employees and joined the CIO.

One of Despres's biggest adventures was traveling with his wife, Marian, to Mexico, where he spent five days socializing and discussing political events with Leon Trotsky. The celebrated Mexican painter Diego Rivera did a portrait of Marian while Leon Despres took Rivera's wife, Frida Kahlo, to a local cinema to watch a French film. "We had a good time. I had no idea she was an icon," Despres recalled six decades later.

During the war years, Despres was exempt from military service because of an old injury, but he continued his work on behalf of unions and civil liberties. He became a member of the Civil Liberties Union of Chicago and later the American Civil Liberties Union (ACLU). After the war, he worked with Mike Myer on several of the projects that Mike Bartell and the SWP had initiated, including desegregating the White City Roller Rink and citywide tenant organizing.

Before the shooting of Coleman, Despres was already familiar with the Hickman case; he had represented the remaining 1733 West Washburne tenants in renters court in June. When Mike Myer asked him to be his cocounsel in the Hickman murder trial, Despres readily agreed— it would be the type of once-in-a-lifetime trial that many criminal defense attorneys never get a shot at. Given the facts of the case, Myer and Despres concurred that they needed to find a prominent Black attorney to join the defense team, someone who was skilled in the courtroom and associated with civil rights activism. William H. Temple was the obvious choice.

Born in Memphis, Temple was raised in Vicksburg, Mississippi, the son of a lawyer and a schoolteacher. He attended Straight University in New Orleans (now Dillard University) and Howard University in Washington, DC. During the First World War, he served in the US Navy and became a commissioned officer. After the war he finished law school at Northwestern University. An ambitious lawyer who eventually became a senior partner at the firm Wimbish & Temple, Temple was active in the NAACP, served as an assistant corporation counsel for the City of Chicago, and was a member of the Metropolitan Community Church. His most famous client was Joe Louis, the world heavyweight boxing champion. His partner C. C. Wimbish was a state senator.

Myer spoke to Temple, and he agreed to join the defense team. Temple was nearly two decades older than Myer and Despres. Impeccably dressed, his hair peppered with gray, Temple brought an air of middle-class respectability and experience to the defense team. Although the court records listed Myer as the lead attorney or chief counsel, Despres remembers that they acted as equals and worked as a team: "We were all chief counsels." All three were well aware of the issues surrounding the Hickman case and were equally aware that the state had a formidable case against their client. All agreed to represent Hickman pro bono.

At their first meeting they had to decide what type of defense they would mount. The state had, at first glance, an airtight case against their client. State's Attorney Sam Freeman had witnesses, the murder weapon, and, most important, Hickman's confession. They couldn't argue self-defense, because Coleman was unarmed when Hickman shot him; further, Coleman's threat to set fire to Hickman's apartment had been made nearly one year earlier, and six months before the fire itself. Despres suggested the defense case include Hickman's state of mind. An insanity defense would allow them to introduce all the issues: Coleman's threats, the fire that killed Hickman's four children, and his deteriorating state of mind. Myer and Despres had spoken to Annie, Willis, and Charles Hickman and developed a clear picture of the decline of James Hickman's mental health in the months leading up his shooting of Coleman. They needed expert testimony to back them up.

On September 18 Myer filed a petition with Judge Charles E. Byrne, the original trial judge in Hickman's case, asking that defense psychiatrists be allowed to examine Hickman. In his petition Myer explained his case in tortured legalese:

That your Petitioner [Myer], together with other counsel for the defendant, have interviewed and conferred with the defendant in the County Jail of Cook County, subsequent thereto, at other places conferred with members of the defendant's family, regarding the facts in the case and mental condition of the defendant; and it is the opinion of your petitioner and counsel, with whom he is associated, that, at the time of the shooting, referred to in the indictments, the defendant was insane.

That, if it should be found, upon trial, the defendant was insane, he would not be guilty of the offense charged in the indictment.

That in order, properly, to prepare the defense of this case, it is necessary that the defendant be examined by qualified and competent psychiatrists, in order that their testimony may be introduced at the trial and defendant's counsel have consulted and arranged for the employment of Dr. Walter A. Adams and Dr. Boris Ury, who are qualified and competent psychiatrists, for the purpose of the defendant and [*sic*] testify at the trial.

Judge Byrne granted the defense's motion and ordered the warden of the Cook County Jail, Frank G. Swain, to allow Adams and Ury to examine Hickman. Hickman's trial was also postponed and eventually rescheduled to begin on November 5 with Judge Rudolf F. Desorts, another veteran judge of the criminal courts, presiding.

Dr. Walter A. Adams, the first Black psychiatrist in Chicago, received his medical degree from Howard University in 1926, having worked summers as a Pullman porter to pay his tuition. He joined the medical faculty at Western Reserve University in Cleveland and later received a grant to study at the Boston Psychopathic Hospital. He moved to Chicago and took up residence at Provident Hospital, the first Black-owned-and-operated hospital in the United States, where he rose to become chief of psychiatry. Dr. Boris Ury, a 1940 graduate of the University of Illinois College of Medicine, was on the faculty of his alma mater as well as the University of Chicago.

Ury conducted a wide-ranging interview with Hickman, asking him questions him about life, his children, the fire, and what happened the day of the shooting of Coleman. Hickman was still deeply distraught by the death of his children, and he emphasized the heartfelt religious pledge he had made to protect them. In his interview with Ury, Hickman kept coming back to the divinely inspired "mission" of his deceased children: "I see the future in these four was destroyed. They would have been great people had they lived. I had a vision, but their lives was cut off."

All parents love their children and see them as special, but Ury was struck by the "grandiose mission" that Hickman believed God had ordained for his children. Hickman told him, "The Lord had work for them to do. He had picked them out." When Ury asked him "whether this godly mission would be confined to work among the colored people . . . he was assured by his client that the mission would be applicable to all people." The death of his children, and the police and state's attorney's lack of interest in it, had produced a deeper trauma for Hickman. Dr. Ury concluded his report by saying that Hickman shot Coleman "in a schizoid, disassociated state, feeling he was accomplishing the Lord's will."

Myer, Despres, and Temple discussed Ury's report. There was no doubt in their minds that this was a significant development in the defense case. It would allow them to argue that Hickman was suffering "temporary insanity" at the time of the shooting of David Coleman and was therefore not responsible for his actions. What had appeared at first glance to be a straightforward revenge killing, one that the police wanted to reduce to a dispute over money, was far more complex. A powerful defense was emerging. How would a jury respond to it?

Several days before the start of the trial, Sam Freeman called Mike Myer at his office. Freeman told him that he wasn't going to seek the death penalty and would ask for only the minimum sentence of fourteen years in prison for Hickman. If Freeman expected Myer to change his client's plea to guilty in exchange for a lighter sentence, he was wrong. Hickman and his lawyers were fighting for an acquittal on all charges.

Myer, Despres, and Temple met with Hickman and explained to him that Freeman was dropping the demand for the death penalty. Immediately the atmosphere surrounding the upcoming trial changed; according to Despres, everything became "less edgy." Myer called Mike Bartell and told him what Freeman had said, and soon the whole defense campaign knew. Hickman's supporters were greatly encouraged. The proposed sentence was a backhanded admission that the pressure of the defense campaign was working. Still, if convicted, Hickman would face at least fourteen years in prison. For a forty-year-old it would be a huge part of his life. A lot was still at stake.

The Hickman Defense Committee wanted to provide a visible show of support for Hickman throughout his trial. On November 5, the first day of the trial, a rally was held on the steps of the courthouse. The sky was overcast and there was a chill in the air. Adorning the face of the building, just above the heads of those attending the rally, were eight allegorical statues of Might, Liberty, Wisdom, Justice, Law, Peace, Truth, and Love, carved by the German sculptor Peter Toneman. Willoughby Abner, wearing a dark full-length overcoat and hat, spoke to the assembled supporters and reporters: "Although James Hickman stands in the defendant's dock today, it is society that is really on trial. Society has created the conditions making Hickman cases and Hickman tragedies inevitable. Society is unconcerned about the loss of Hickman's children; unconcerned about the miserable housing conditions that Hickman and his family of nine had to live under. The same government which failed to heed the need of Hickman and millions of other Hickmans is now trying to convict Hickman for its own crimes, its own failures." Abner then led the assembled crowd into the building.

Judge Desorts's courtroom exuded authority and solemnity with its dim lighting, dark paneling, and hardwood seating. The judge's bench towered over everyone. The acoustics were terrible. Voices didn't carry well; it was hard to hear anyone, including the judge on his high perch. Witnesses had to project their voices to be heard by counsel and the jury. It was even worse for the audience. Not only was hearing the testimony difficult, but sitting on the hard pews, even for a short period, was highly uncomfortable.

Hickman's supporters entered as a group and filled most of the pews. Frank Fried, Mike Bartell, Sidney Lens, Charles Chiakulas, and Willoughby Abner sat directly behind the defense's table and kept a constant vigil during the trial. Lens later remembered that the trial was a "dramatic affair that attracted considerable attention." Everyone was nervous with anticipation.

James Hickman was already sitting at the defense table with his lawyers. His surviving family was also in attendance; all of them, with the exception of his daughter Arlene, were expected to testify.

During the course of the trial, Hickman's routine was the same each day. He got up, had breakfast, and put on his suit. He was taken to the basement of the jail and handcuffed with all the other inmates that were to appear in court that day. Escorted by guards, they were walked as a group through an underground tunnel to the criminal court building, and each was deposited in the appropriate courtroom for a trial or a hearing. The guards would remove Hickman's handcuffs once he was with his attorneys. The process was reversed at the end of the day.

After Judge Desorts entered the room, *The People of the State of Illinois v. James Hickman*, case 47–1659, was called to order. The dreary process of jury selection began. Prospective jurors had been drawn from the voter registration list. Cook County was overwhelmingly white, and given the number of challenges allowed to the prosecution, Leon Despres didn't think it would be possible to get even one Black man or woman on the jury.

Nevertheless, there was one surprise during jury selection. After a man was accepted by both the prosecution and the defense, Chiakulas leaned over to Lens and whispered in his ear: "Holy Christ, that's one of my best shop stewards they just put on." Chiakulas had had no way of knowing that one of his stewards would be selected, and he had no contact with him during the course of the trial, but after the trial was over, this man provided some inside information on the jury's thinking. Only later was it discovered that the mistress of a prosecution witness had also been selected. By the end of three days, six white men and six white women had been chosen for the jury. There was a weekend break before opening arguments took place on Monday morning, November 10.

Sam Freeman may have dropped his demand for the death penalty, but he vigorously prosecuted the case. In his opening, he argued that James Hickman had broken the law and needed to be punished for taking another man's life. Hickman's killing of David Coleman was "premeditated" and done with "malice aforethought." Freeman wanted a conviction.

In his opening statement, Mike Myer argued that Hickman was not guilty because he was "temporarily insane" at the time of the shooting and his illness was well within the legal definition of insanity. The real victims in this tragedy were James Hickman and his family.

The prosecution presented its case first. Freedman introduced into evidence the Mauser .32-caliber blue steel automatic pistol used to shoot Coleman, along with Hickman's confession. He called eight witnesses, including Coleman's wife Sylvestra and four police officers. Each gave testimony that was virtually identical to what they had given at the coroner's inquest. Percy C. Brown, David Coleman's half-brother, and Charles McLaurin, the two eyewitnesses to the shooting, also took the stand. During Freeman's examination of Brown and McLaurin, he sought to refute Hickman's claim that Coleman had confessed to setting the fire that killed his children. But under intense cross-examination by William Temple, both reluctantly admitted that they had not been close enough to hear the exchange between Hickman and Coleman.

Myer opened the defense's case by calling Julia Rogers and Will Jackson, tenants at 1733 West Washburne along with their families. They testified that Coleman had threatened to burn the tenants out. Then Willis Hickman testified about seeing Coleman in the building the night before the fire and about his father's deteriorating mental health.

Next it was Annie Hickman's turn on the stand. She was a petite and very thin woman, with a thin face and a sharp chin. Her hair was pulled back in a bun, giving her a slightly stern look. With tears in her eyes she told of the fire that had taken the lives of her children. She told the jury that after their first child was born, her husband had heard "a voice from above" that had charged him with "protecting and keeping his family together." She said that he had made a vow to God to do so and had repeated his vow over the years.

All eyes were on the most important defense witness, James Hickman, when he took the stand after his wife. An onlooker in the courtroom that day would have seen an oval-faced man with wire-rimmed glasses and a neatly trimmed mustache, a thin body of medium height with a strength that came from years of hard work, and a naturally friendly demeanor. Wearing a gray suit with a white flower in its lapel, he spoke in a calm, low voice, recounting his life in Mississippi and his journey to and struggles in Chicago. Despres thought that his language was "poetic," shaped by the Bible that had guided his life.

"My feelings was that I was mistreated without cause," he told the court. "I felt that my children was without guardian, that they suffered death, that they ought to be free on land and living. This was God fixed this. I had raised these children up and God knowed that vow I made to him . . . that these children was to be raised up. God wasn't pleased what happed to them."

Myer asked him to describe his life between the fire and the shooting of Coleman six months later. He responded: "I had two sons and two daughters who would some day be great men and someday they would have married, someday they would have been fathers and mothers of children; these children would have children and then these children would have children and generation of Hickmans could raise up and enjoy peace."

Having told the jury of his "contract with God," Hickman said that after learning of the fate of his children, he heard a "voice demanding that he fulfill his contract." He told the jury that he resisted this voice for a long time but on July 16 he finally went to confront Coleman. He shot Coleman twice before Coleman confessed, and then shot him twice more.

Hickman was on the stand all day Thursday and for an hour on the following morning. Freeman did his best to discredit him but failed. Despres considered Hickman's testimony on the stand "magnificent."

The last witnesses for the defense were Hickman's pastor, who testified to his good character, and Dr. Adams and Dr. Ury, who reported on their examination of James Hickman. The prosecution provided no psychiatric testimony to refute that of the defense psychiatrists, which was a huge blunder.

William Temple and Leon Despres made the closing arguments for the defense. Having argued that the testimony presented by the prosecution had been either refuted or seriously challenged, they proceeded into a scathing, wide-ranging attack on the housing conditions that Black Americans had suffered. Temple and Despres asked the jury to find James Hickman not guilty.

Freeman, trying to make up for lost ground, made a hysterical appeal to the jury, calling Hickman a cold-blooded killer and stressing the need for "upholding our constitution, our way of life, and our civilization." He tried to undermine the defense psychiatrists' testimony by mocking them: "These men don't know any more about what goes on in a man's head than my two-year-old granddaughter." It was not a good performance.

Judge Desorts gave the jury its instructions, and it went into deliberation. Behind closed doors, the jury of six men and six women chose a woman, Regina Zajfert, as the jury foreman. The trial had lasted nine days from the jury selection to the closing arguments. The jury deliberated for six and a half hours on Friday and for twelve and a half hours on Saturday. They took eight closely divided votes before Zajfert informed the judge that they could not arrive at a verdict.

Why did the jury vote the way it did? After the trial, Chiakulas's union steward told Bartell that at the beginning of deliberations one of the male jury members had said, "Before they send Hickman to the chair, they'll have to send me there." While Hickman wasn't facing execution, this man appeared to have strongly identified with him. Bartell thought *all* the male jury members were working-class people who could identify with Hickman's difficulty providing for his family.

The jury was divided, seven for acquittal, five for conviction—a "hung jury." All six of the men and one of the women voted for acquittal. Judge Desorts declared a mistrial. Freeman announced that the state would retry Hickman.

Short of an outright acquittal, a hung jury was the next best thing for James Hickman, but it did raise the prospect of having to go through another trial and renewing the defense campaign. Myer, Despres, Temple, and members of the executive committee of the Hickman Defense Committee met to decide what to do next. Bartell was optimistic. For him the hung jury was "encouraging, since it would indicate, assuming this to be an average jury, that it will be very difficult for the state to get a unanimous vote for conviction the second time. We believe that it is quite possible, if not probable, that the second trial will end in a hung jury again." He was thinking long term. "The nature of the case is such that it is likely that there will be strong opinions both ways. A second hung jury will put us in a powerful position to wage a pressure campaign on the state to release Hickman."

But Bartell soon shifted gears, choosing to put pressure on the State's Attorney's Office to drop the case. The circumstances weren't likely to get much better than they were. Fried had already traveled across the country, setting up defense committees in many cities in anticipation of a probable national campaign for Hickman's freedom. So the Hickman Defense Committee sent out a call for letters from supporters across the country demanding that the state's attorney drop the case. "I think the general popular sympathy that we had generated affected the State's Attorney's Office," Lens recalled.

Freeman called Myer and offered him a face-saving deal. He proposed dropping the murder charge if Hickman would plead guilty to manslaughter. He would recommend to Judge Desorts that Hickman be sentenced to two years' probation. Myer spoke to Hickman, and they agreed to accept the offer.

Standing before Judge Desorts, Freeman told the judge that one of the major reasons his office didn't want a retrial was the public support for Hickman that had emerged across the country. He held up letters of support, resolutions, and telegrams. "They are too numerous to read all of them here," Freeman declared, "but the general opinion is to the effect that mercy ought to be shown to an individual who, under the stress of the loss of four children, has been punished to such an extent that society can be magnanimous and afford him a chance to return to his remaining children and his wife, and spend the rest of his lifetime in peace." Although "some quarters" would disagree with his recommendation, Freeman concluded, "the state feels this man has paid enough with the loss of his children."

A smiling, elated James Hickman walked out of court a free man on December 16, 1947. He had served five months in jail. Members of the Hickman Defense Committee, including Mike Bartell, joined his lawyers on the steps of courthouse and took several photographs with James and Annie Hickman. This was the last time that any of them, with the exception of Mike Myer, would ever see the Hickmans again. The Hickman family returned to their private lives.

"Work is all they look for you to do."

Epilogue
"It was done at wrong time. Stupid."

The fire began on the back porch and spread upward, consuming the two-story home at 3034 South Forty-Eighth Street Court in Cicero, a suburb just west of Chicago. It was Sunday morning, Valentine's Day 2010, a day for celebrating love and affection, when the blaze took the lives of seven people. Among the dead were Byron Reed, his girlfriend, Sallie Gist, and their two sons, Rayshawn Reed, who was three years old, and newborn Brian, just three days old. Sallie's sixteen-year-old twin brother and sister, Elijah and Elisha, and a family friend, Tiera Davison, eighteen years old, also died in the fire. When Cicero firefighters arrived on the scene, they could hear smoke detectors blaring, but it was too late. Two bodies were found near the back porch door, while the four children had died trapped in the attic; relatives of the deceased said they had been sleeping up there. Before the roof collapsed, firefighters found a box spring in the attic.

There were no fire escapes, and the deadly attic was connected to the second-floor kitchen by a single stairwell that was blocked by fire on that fateful Valentine's Day. It was the deadliest fire in the greater Chicago area in many years and raised concerns about overcrowded housing in Cicero. "The attic is a concern if it was being occupied for living quarters," Cicero trustee Dennis Raleigh told the *Chicago Tribune*. "There was only one exit. If people were up there, they shouldn't have been." Neighbors believed that somewhere between twenty and thirty people had been living in the building at the time of the fire. The building's owner, Lawrence Myers, and maintenance man, Marion Comier, watched the firefighters put out the conflagration. Before the fire, according to unnamed witnesses, Myers and Comier were acting strangely and saying suspicious things to one another.

Cicero police asked an unnamed witness to wear a wire and try to get Myers and Comier to talk about the cause of the fire, and the witness agreed. It worked. "I had my mitts in it if that's what you want to hear," Comier told the witness. He explained how he had set the fire using oil. "I dumped it on there," Comier boasted, "threw a match and that was it. . . . I thought this shit out." Myers was reportedly having trouble with the Internal Revenue Service and had told Comier he would pay him to "take care of the building." Myers allegedly wanted the insurance money. He was recorded saying: "It was done at wrong time. Stupid. I didn't want him to hurt anyone." Myers and Cormier were charged with seven counts of first-degree murder and two counts of aggravated arson. They pleaded not guilty.

The underlying issues in the Hickman case clearly have not gone away. But the story itself has. How can such a powerful story disappear from the public memory? After all, the Hickman story features not only rapacious greed and racism and an excruciatingly painful family tragedy but also the triumph of justice over very long odds. It was set not in some remote part of the country but in Chicago, whose crime-obsessed tabloid press frequently salivates over stories of much less interest.

Several factors combined over the years to keep the Hickman case from getting the recognition that it deserves. The events took place in

1947. Over the next few years the dark grip of the Cold War would tighten around society in the United States. A virulent level of repression would drive socialists, communists, and radicals to the margins of American society. In many ways, the campaign to save James Hickman was one of the last echoes of the great radicalization of the American working class in the 1930s. A successful campaign by revolutionary socialists to free an African American man who had shot and killed his landlord was not the type of story to be highlighted at the zenith of the American Century. The Hickman case was steamrolled by a decade and half of political repression and cultural conformity.

This, however, is only a part of the answer. Another important reason for the disappearance of this story is because of those who have written the history of the American left. By and large, these historians were members of the Communist Party or the New Left in the 1960s, and few of them have shown any interest in or political sympathy for the revolutionary tradition of Marxism and the real history of the Russian Revolution in the current of Trotskyism in the United States in the 1930s and 1940s. There are notable exceptions, such as Alan Wald's *The New York Intellectuals* and Bryan Palmer's *James P. Cannon and the Origins of the American Revolutionary Left, 1890–1928*, but too often the most popular histories of the left in the 1930s and 1940s simply dismiss, denigrate, or omit the role of Trotskyists in the radical movement. One of the most blatant examples of this is *Labor's Untold Story* by Richard O. Boyer and Herbert M. Morais, published by the United Electrical, Radio and Machine Workers of America (UE), one of the CIO unions led by the Communist Party. It ignores, for example, the Trotskyist-led Minneapolis Teamster strike of 1934, even though this was one of three strikes (the others being the Toledo Auto-Lite strike and the San Francisco general strike) that directly led to the formation of the CIO.

Such distortions arising from silence may be extreme, but they are not uncommon. The 1941 trial of the Trotskyists of the Socialist Workers Party for "sedition" under the reactionary Smith Act became the model for the trials that destroyed the Communist Party after the Second World

War. Yet as Ellen Schrecker notes in her *Many Are the Crimes: McCarthyism in America*, "There is little scholarship on the Trotskyist Smith Act case. While recognizing its implications for the later Smith Act cases, most writers tend to dismiss it in a sentence or two." Isn't it time that Trotskyism receive the proper recognition it deserves for its role in American radical history?

There are many stories like the Hickman case that need to be recovered from oblivion and retold. Clint Eastwood's 2008 film *Changeling*, set in Los Angeles in 1928, told the real-life story of Christine Collins and her search for the truth about the kidnapping of her son and the mind-boggling public relations evasion by the Los Angeles Police Department, which returned to her the wrong child and then attempted to silence her when she refused to go along with its "mistake." The LAPD's cover-up of its mistake led to an explosion of public protest. The story disappeared from public memory for eight decades, however, until the screenwriter J. Michael Straczynski, a former journalist, was contacted by an old source at Los Angeles city hall, who told him the city was planning to destroy some of its archives and there was "something [he] should see." This turned out to be a transcript of a city council hearing relating to Collins's case.

There are thousands of stories of injustice hidden away in the archives of city halls around the country. Hopefully, a new generation of journalists and historians can bring to light many of them before they are lost in the mists of history.

Driving south on Martin Luther King Jr. Drive past Twenty-Fifth Street, one enters Bronzeville, Chicago's best-known historic Black neighborhood. Right in the middle of the road looms a fifteen-foot statue of a poor traveler, an African American man holding in his left hand a suitcase held together by rope and raising his right hand to point north. This is Alison Saar's *Monument to the Great Northern Migration*. Dedicated in 1996 by the City of Chicago, it commemorates the tens of thousands of Black southern migrants who came to Chicago in search of a better life.

There are no monuments commemorating the tragedies that befell many of them when they got here. There are no monuments commemorating the twenty-three African Americans killed during the 1919 Chicago Race Riot or those who died in the needless fires of 1947.

Ben Shahn's artwork inspired by the Hickman tragedy has survived. In the early 1960s Leon Despres bought Shahn's *Hickman Story* illustrations from the Downtown Gallery in New York City for sixteen monthly installments of twenty-five dollars. Shahn had exhibited his work at the Downtown Gallery over many decades. For his part, Despres had been elected the alderman from Chicago's Hyde Park ward in 1955. He hung Shahn's illustrations on the wall of his law office in the Loop. When John Culhane, a *Chicago Daily News* political reporter, asked him why he had them there, Despres told him: "To remind me of the conditions of housing in Chicago and what can result. I don't know what these children would have become, but I do know the hopes their parents had for them. The Hickman children remind me to work so that other lives and other hopes aren't cut off."

Appendix
John Bartlow Martin, Ben Shahn, and the Hickman Story

On March 25, 1947, an explosion ripped through Centralia Number 5 coal mine, ending the lives of 111 miners. Centralia was sixty-five miles east of St. Louis and a five-hour drive from Chicago. It was not some wretched company town isolated in the mountains of West Virginia or Kentucky, but a comfortable, pleasant-looking small city surrounded by farms on the plains. The miners, members of the United Mine Workers of America (UMWA), had been warning for years about the dangerous working conditions in the mines, particularly the constant buildup of coal dust, which could easily explode with deadly consequences. A year before the explosion, William E. Rowenkampf, the recording secretary of Local 52 of UMWA, had written a letter to Illinois governor Dwight H. Green, a Republican with national political ambitions, outlining the dangerous conditions and asking for help: "This is a plea to you, to please save our lives, to please make the department of mines and minerals enforce the laws at the no. 5 of the Centralia Coal Co. before we have a dust explosion at this mine like just happened in Kentucky and West Virginia."

Rowenkampf's plea was ignored. In the disaster, sixty-five miners burned to death; another forty-five died from a mix of toxic gases 540 feet below the surface. Thirty-one miners escaped, and eight were rescued. Of the rescued miners, one later died. It was a devastating event for Centralia and the surrounding community.

John Bartlow Martin had been a writer for some years then, having honed his writing skills after starting out as a cub reporter for Indiana newspapers, then working for true crime magazines, and finally writing regularly for *Harper's*. *Harper's* was one of the "big slicks," the glossy weekly magazines that included the *New Yorker*, the *Atlantic*, *Colliers*, and the *Saturday Review of Literature*, during the heyday of magazine journalism in the 1940s and '50s.

Born in 1915, Martin had spent most of his childhood on Brookeside Avenue in an Indianapolis neighborhood whose best years were behind it. His mother was an adherent of Christian Science, a sect known for hostility to doctors and not providing medicine to the ill. Martin's two younger brothers died when they were, respectively, six months and five years old. Once an adult, he was almost certain that his youngest brother's life could have been saved with medical attention. His mother's hostility to medicine was rivaled only by her hostility to Catholicism. When he was very young, John's mother warned him that Catholics deliberately build their churches on hilltops because it was from such "military strong-points" that they would take over the country.

Martin's father, John Sr., was a remote man who had quit school at thirteen to go to work. He started out as a carpenter and rose to become a construction contractor. During his father's prosperous days in the 1920s, Martin remembered, he would drive his big blue Buick into the heart of Indianapolis's Black community, looking for workers. He would pull up in front of a pool hall where a crowd of men were hanging out and shout, "Which one of you niggers wants to go to work on Monday?"

The Ku Klux Klan controlled the "prosperous" Indiana of the 1920s. "Some of my early boyhood memories are watching a seemingly endless parade of robed and hooded Klansmen marching around Monument Circle in Indianapolis in dead silence." During the 1930s his father's business was wiped out. Martin remembered on at least one occasion accompanying his father to a factory gate early in the morning to look for work and seeing the factory foreman come out and hang a "No Help Wanted" sign. The Great Depression cast a long shadow over almost everyone's life.

Young John Martin's interest in literature and writing, along with his sensitivity toward human suffering, was sparked by a high school teacher who turned him on to Hemingway, Dos Passos, and others and by a working-class high school friend who was a member of the Young Communist League.

From the very beginning of his research on Centralia, Martin wanted to "fix responsibility for the disaster." The scale of death and misery was overwhelming; Martin had never covered a story like this before, and it caused him some discomfort. "Had I the right to question a coal miner's widow?" After overcoming his initial discomfort, he conducted extensive interviews with the surviving miners and their families. "I did not want the story to turn to into a debate among the powerful—Governor Green, John L. Lewis of the UMWA, and the coal company. I wanted it to be the miners' story."

Martin went to Springfield, the capital of Illinois, examined the files of the Department of Mines and Minerals, and found extensive reports on Centralia's unsafe conditions, all dutifully stamped and filed away. "Seldom has a major catastrophe of any kind been blueprinted so accurately so far in advance." *Harper's* published "The Blast in Centralia No. 5: A Mine Disaster No One Stopped" in March 1948 to coincide with the one-year anniversary of the disaster. At more than 18,500 words, the story was the longest ever published in the magazine. *Harper's* commissioned Ben Shahn, a noted artist best known for his work *The Passion of Sacco and Vanzetti*, to provide illustrations for the Centralia story. Shahn's artwork and Martin's prose raised the quality of the story above standard journalism. Martin's Centralia article caused a stir and was credited with helping to bring about a new federal mine safety law. After his many years of hard work, John Bartlow Martin was recognized as a writer of national importance.

As he was completing his article on the Centralia mine disaster, Martin had been reading about the Hickman case. When he proposed a story on the case to the editors of *Harper's*, they commissioned him to write it.

"Though the case's background is not unusual, I know of no other where the issue was so clear cut and the events subsequent to the fire so dramatic," Martin wrote to the *Harper's* editors. "Moreover, the background makes it possible to widen the meaning of the story from the particular to the general. It really is an important story. It is the story of crime produced by a sociological problem, a crime seen in its social context. I see it as a peg on which to hang an account of tenement housing and population pressure among Negroes in the North during the postwar period."

A few days before Martin interviewed the Hickmans, he drove to the neighborhood where the fire had taken place to get a feel for it. Martin thought the Near West Side neighborhood was quickly deteriorating into a dangerous slum area.

"The best buildings are the churches and the factories," he noted. "The buildings where people live are high brick tenements, patched-up wooden tenements, sheds. In between are vast wastelands, desolate areas where buildings have collapsed or been torn down, the excavations partly filled with rubble." The front doors of apartment buildings stood wide open; anyone could walk in. Mary Adams still owned the 1733 West Washburne building, though all the tenants from the previous year had moved. Martin had a few names of neighbors who had witnessed the tragic events but wasn't sure whether any of them still lived in the area. The neighbor who had broken the news of the death of his children to James Hickman, however, was still there, and he agreed to talk to Martin but wished to remain anonymous.

Martin liked interviewing people in their own homes. They generally felt comfortable surrounded by the family photographs, mementos, and souvenirs representing their personal history. Sitting in someone's living room gave one a deeper feeling for what was important to them, what they took pride in, and sometimes even what they had lost over time. When he knocked on the door of the Hickmans' modest, attached one-story home on the South Side of Chicago, it had been over a year and a half since the fire that had killed their four youngest children. When Annie and James Hickman welcomed him in, Martin left his notepad and pen in his jacket pocket. He had learned from past experience that producing them at the beginning of an interview could put people off or even frighten them. Introducing himself, he explained that he wanted to tell the story of their family's trek from Mississippi to Chicago and the disaster that devastated their family, and he wanted to focus in particular on the odyssey of James Hickman.

"The Hickman Story" was published in the August 1948 edition of *Harper's*. It provided the widest national exposure that the Hickman case received at the time. The article was one of those gems of magazine writing that combine the clarity of journalism with the skill of a novelist to sketch the personalities of the characters involved. Further, lifting the story off the pages and deepening the reader's experience were sixteen accompanying illustrations by Ben Shahn, one of the most celebrated artists of the day.

He was born Benjamin Shahn in 1898 in Lithuania, when it was part of the Russian empire; his father, Joshua Hessel, had been exiled to Siberia by the czarist government. But Hessel escaped from Siberia and made his way to the United States via South Africa. Shahn's mother, Gittel, gathered up the rest of the family and immigrated to New York City in 1906, reuniting with her husband. Shahn spent his youth in New York City; his talent as an artist was apparent early on and was encouraged by his schoolteachers as well as his father. He was first trained as a lithographer and a graphic designer. He entered New York University as biology major in 1919, but in 1921 he transferred to the City College of New York and the National Academy of Design to study art. In the mid- and late 1920s he traveled throughout North Africa and Europe with his first wife, studying the traditional art of North Africa as well as the great masters of Europe. He struggled to develop his own style.

By the 1930s he had settled on a realistic painting style that he hoped would help to promote social change. "I hate injustice; I guess that's about the only thing I really do hate," he once told an interviewer. Shahn had a strong, domineering personality. His friend Walker Evans, the famed photographer, said, "All he had to do was to come into the room and you felt tired." John Bartlow Martin recalled, however, that Shahn had "the kindest eyes" he had ever seen. His first big success was *The Passion of Sacco and Vanzetti*, twenty-three paintings depicting the life-and-death struggles of the two Italian immigrant anarchists who were framed and executed for murder in Massachusetts in 1927. Shahn had followed the trial while traveling in Europe and had witnessed a demonstration of twenty thousand in Paris opposing Sacco and Vanzetti's execution. Exhibited at the Downtown Gallery in New York City in 1932, *The Passion* was praised by the world-famous Mexican muralist Diego Rivera as being "as moving as anything of the kind I have ever seen."

The Downtown Gallery was established and owned by Edith Gregor Halpert and Berthe Kroll Goldsmith for the purpose of promoting modern American art. Halpert had become its sole owner in 1935.

Shahn moved on to do a sixteen-painting series relating to the persecution of Tom Mooney, a socialist union activist framed for the bombing of a war preparedness parade in San Francisco in 1916. Ten people died in the bombing. The exhibition of Shahn's Tom Mooney paintings did not garner the same acclaim as his Sacco and Vanzetti series, but Rivera once again praised his work: "Shahn's series on the Mooney case is even stronger and of finer quality than his Sacco-Vanzetti paintings."

Rivera had been commissioned by the Rockefeller family to paint a fresco in the main lobby of Rockefeller Center, the very symbol of the Rockefeller corporate empire, in New York City. The painting, *Man at the Crossroads Looking with Hope and High Vision to the Choosing of a New and Better Future*, was to be completed by the time of the center's grand opening in fall 1932. Shahn joined the team of artists assisting Rivera with his masterwork. Rivera depicted the crossroads as humanity leaving capitalism behind and marching toward socialism, replete with a portrait of the Russian revolutionary leader Vladimir Lenin.

The building managers were very curious as the painting of the fresco advanced, as they had been told only in the haziest of terms what it was to depict. Their curiosity turned to panic and hostility after the head of Lenin appeared. Nelson Rockefeller wrote a letter to Rivera asking him to remove Lenin ("might easily seriously offend a great many people"). Rivera replied that he was willing to "find an acceptable solution to the problem you raise." But he was willing to go only so far. Shahn, for his part, threatened to organize a strike among the assistants if Rivera capitulated.

Rockefeller did not reply to Rivera's letter; instead, Rockefeller's men soon expelled Rivera and his team of artists from the building and constructed a plywood cover for the still unfinished fresco. Shahn organized protests involving hundreds of artists, but to no avail. In one of the great crimes against art in modern history, the fresco was destroyed.

Shahn relied heavily on photographs and talking to people in order to produce some of his best-known work. Having not been personally present during the events surrounding Sacco and Vanzetti or Tom Mooney, he had become interested in photography. He was hired by the federal government's Resettlement Agency to document the agency's work to alleviate the difficult conditions of farmers in the South. Shahn's "emphasis was on people rather than landscapes or architectural sites. He showed a special gift for creating series of photos, resulting in a near cinematic effect," according to his biographer and friend Howard Greenfeld. During the Second World War, Shahn worked for the Office of War Information, producing posters for the Allied war against the Nazis. One poster showed a man with a giant hood over his head with his hands cuffed, and the words "This is Nazi Brutality."

By the mid-1940s, Shahn had become one of the most famous artists in the United States. In recognition of his importance, the Museum of

Modern Art in New York held a retrospective of his work on September 30, 1947. He was the youngest painter in the museum's history to be honored in such a manner. He continued to do work for a variety of well-known magazines, including *Harper's*.

When he was approached about illustrating Martin's Hickman story, he agreed and entered into long discussions with Martin about the case and the people involved in it. The story touched him deeply, and he struggled to capture the enormity of the Hickman family tragedy:

> I was asked to make drawings for the story and, after several discussions with the writer, felt that I had gained enough of the feel of the situation to proceed. I examined a great deal of the factual visual material, and then I discarded all of it. It seemed to me the implications of this event transcended the immediate story; there was universality about man's dread of fire, and his sufferings from fire. There was a universality in the pity which such a disaster invokes. . . . And the relentless poverty which had pursued this man, and which dominated the story, had its own kind of universality.
>
> Sometimes, if one is particularly satisfied with a piece of work which he has completed, he may say to himself, "well done," and go on to something else. Not in this instance, however. I found that I could not dismiss the event about which I had made drawings—the so-called "Hickman Story." . . . I had some curious sense of responsibility about it, a sort of personal involvement.

The Hickman tragedy "aroused in me," Shahn recalled, "a chain of personal memories."

> There were two great fires in my own childhood, one only colorful, the other disastrous and unforgettable. Of the first, I remember only that the Russian village in which my grandfather lived burned, and I was there. I remember the excitement, the flames breaking out everywhere. . . . The other fire left its mark upon me and all my family, and left scars on my father's hand and face, for he had clambered up a drainpipe and taken each of my brothers and sisters and me over the house one by one, burning himself painfully in the process. Meanwhile our house and all belongings were consumed, and my parents stricken beyond their power to recover.

The most powerful of all of Shahn's Hickman drawings is of the four huddled, deceased Hickman children. Shahn's "personal involvement" led him to use his own siblings as the basis for his image: "they resemble much more closely my own brothers and sisters." *Harper's* published sixteen of Shahn's illustrations with Martin's article. The series has an epic feel.

A Note on Sources

I have had to piece this story together from a variety of sources. Only two of the major figures in it are still alive. Frank Fried lost almost everything he had related to the Hickman case, except some photographs, in the great Oakland fire of late 1991. James and Annie's son Willis Hickman lives on the West Side of Chicago. Of course, both Frank and Willis still have memories of those traumatic events in 1947.

My most important and most surprising source of information, however, has been the transcripts of hearings conducted by the Cook County coroner. Until the mid-1970s, coroners in Illinois conducted inquests that involved hearings, subpoenaed witnesses, and took sworn testimony. The Cook County coroner conducted four wide-ranging hearings into the deaths of the four Hickman children. The transcripts of the "Inquest on the Bodies of Sylvester Hickman, Velvana [*sic*] Hickman, Elzana [*sic*] Hickman and Lester Hickman" provided much of the primary material for my understanding of the living conditions of the Hickmans and the events leading up to and including the fire that killed them. The coroner's inquests were also a major source of primary material into the deaths of the children of the White family, Albert Hill, the Phillipses' brother, the Ohio Street fire victims, and David Coleman's activities.

The Chicago Police Department's reports and records on their investigation of the death of Coleman, including James Hickman's confession, was another crucial source of information. These and the coroner's inquests are the only official records documenting the tragedies that took the victims' lives. These records are invaluable sources of information on the tragic deaths of working-class people and the horrible conditions they lived in. They are records that need to be preserved for future generations.

Neil R. McMillen's classic *Dark Journey: Black Mississippians in the Age of Jim Crow* was enormously helpful in portraying sharecropping life in the Mississippi Delta. I found the early history of Winston County documented at http://winston.msgen.info/townsschools/townsschools.htm (the county's website). *Always Bring a Crowd! The Story of Frank Lumpkin, Steelworker* by Beatrice Lumpkin provided the corporate history of Wisconsin Steel and the working conditions of Black steelworkers. *Land of Hope* by James Grossman and *The Promised Land* by Christopher Lemann provided important background information on the Black migration to Chicago. Lea Demarest Taylor's papers at the University of Illinois at Chicago helped provide crucial information concerning the victims and aftermath of the Ohio Street fire.

John Bartlow Martin, Sidney Lens, and Leon Despres left many more records. Martin's work published in *Harper's* was most important for this book. "The Blast in Centralia No. 5," "The Hickman Story," "Incident at Fernwood," and his autobiography *It Seems Like Only Yesterday: Memoirs of Writing, Presidential Politics, and Diplomatic Life* were crucial sources. I could not have written this book without the coroner's hearing records and Martin's "The Hickman Story," based on a long interview with James and Annie Hickman. Martin's autobiography, as one might expect from a journalist, reveals much about the influences on his early life and about his views and his methods of research and writing. His obituaries in the *New York Times* and the *Chicago Tribune* were also very useful.

Sidney Lens was a prolific writer and historian. His autobiography *Unrepentant Radical* provided me with much information about his family history, his life as a young radical, his contributions to the Hickman defense campaign, and his observations on the Hickman murder trial. His papers preserved at the Chicago History Museum contain the only surviving material relating to the Hickman defense campaign, including leaflets, posters, correspondence, and a copy of the speech he wrote for Tallulah Bankhead.

Leon Despres's memoir, *Challenging the Daley Machine*, written with Kenan Heise, and Heise's interviews with Despres in *Chicago Afternoons with Leon: 99½ Years Old and Looking Forward*, informed me about Despres's early life growing up in Hyde Park. He discusses the role he played in the aftermath of the Memorial Day massacre in a video presentation, *Beyond Haymarket and Pullman: Mapping Chicago's Working Class Struggles*. Despres's thoughts about the strategy of the Hickman legal defense team were given in my interview with him when he was one hundred years old at his home in Hyde Park in November 2009.

"A Lifetime for Socialism," published in the magazine *Against the Current*, by Karin Baker and Patrick M. Quinn provided a very useful outline of Mike Bartell's life, and Frank Fried's memories of Bartell's daily routine and style of political leadership filled in the gaps. Karin Baker and Jelger Kalmijn took time out from their busy schedules, rummaged through their respective attics, and found three hours of recorded interviews with Bartell and some of his personal papers, which proved invaluable in documenting his early life. Robert Cohen's *When the Old Left Was Young: Student Radicals and America's First Mass Student Movement, 1929–1941* was very useful for sketching Bartell's years at the City College of New York. Linda Myer provided me with her father's notes on their family history and the harrowing escape from czarist Russia, and an excerpt from "From the Czarist Underground" by Mark Khinoy, a short history of the maternal side of her family. Linda also provided me with three copies of eulogies given at her father's funeral by his law partner and closest friends. The FBI files on Mike Bartell, Edith Zaslow, Mike Myer, and Belle Myer proved to be important sources of information on their work and political life. The FBI's criminal spying on their perfectly legal activities, however, cannot be condoned.

My knowledge of the history of American Trotskyism and the importance of political defense campaigns in the radical tradition in the United States is largely from James Cannon's *The First Ten Years of American Communism* and *Socialism on Trial*, Bryan Palmer's *James P. Cannon and the Origins of the American Revolutionary Left, 1890–1928*, and Albert Goldman's *In Defense of Socialism*. Alan M. Wald's epic book *The New York Intellectuals: The Rise and Decline of the Anti-Stalinist Left from the 1930s to the 1980s* is a must read for understanding American Trotskyism in the 1930s and 1940s. Patrick M. Quinn provided me with a thick folder of material relating to Albert Goldman and a biography he wrote of the long-neglected Goldman. *Traditions and Guiding Ideas of the SWP in Defense Activities* by George Novack was very useful. My discussions with Joel Geier were also very important.

Matt Nichter took time out from researching his own dissertation to search the Socialist Workers Party archives at the Wisconsin Historical Society for anything related to the SWP's work on the Hickman case. He found important reports by the Chicago SWP branch on tenant organizing, civil rights activism, and the Hickman case; these were of immense assistance. The SWP's newspaper, the *Militant*, proved an important reference, especially the many articles written by Robert Birchman from 1945 through 1947, which chronicled the rising level of racist violence, fire bombings, and tenement fires suffered by Black Chicagoans during this period and the efforts of the SWP to organize campaigns against them. "The Case of James Hickman" by Robert Birchman, published in the SWP's magazine, the *Fourth International*, includes a useful summary of the Hickman case. Art Preis's *Labor's Giant Step* and Sharon Smith's *Subterranean Fire* supplied important background information on the labor struggles I have touched on throughout this book.

One of the great pleasures of doing the research for this book has been rediscovering the history of Black Chicago. *Black Metropolis: A Study of Negro Life in a Northern City* by Horace Cayton and St. Clair Drake withstands the test of time and was a great source of information on housing and race in the 1930s and 1940s. James R. Grossman's *Land of Hope: Chicago, Black Southerners, and the Great Migration* informed me on the role of the *Chicago Defender* in encouraging Black migration to the North, and what Blacks found upon their arrival.

Roi Ottley's *Lonely Warrior: The Life and Times of Robert S. Abbott, Founder of the "Chicago Defender" Newspaper* provided excellent background material for understanding the creation of the Bud Billiken character. *Forum for Protest: The Black Press during World War II*, by Lee Finkle, furnished more general information on the *Chicago Defender.*

The *Chicago Defender* itself, both its Chicago and national editions, was one of the very best sources of material on the housing conditions and the menace of fires in Chicago's Black community. It was one of the leading voices of Black America during the 1940s. The *Defender*'s reporters chronicled the hopes, struggles, and tragedies of Black Chicago. During the fire crisis it documented the ongoing catastrophe while trying to put a stop to it.

Ten Million Black Voices, with Richard Wright's magnificent, angry prose and photos edited by Edwin Rosskam, illustrated the scourge that kitchenette apartments were for the Black residents of Chicago. Horace Cayton's autobiography *Long Old Road* revealed the behind-the-scenes battles during the Ohio Street fire investigation, as well as his life in Chicago. Vernon Jarrett's contribution to *My Soul Looks Back in Wonder: Voices of the Civil Rights Experience* and his articles in the *Chicago Defender* offer insights into his life and the violent events that occurred during the integration of Airport Homes. Arnold R. Hirsch's *The Making of the Second Ghetto: Race and Housing in Chicago, 1940–1960* and his "Martin H. Kennelly: The Mugwump and the Machine" in *The Mayors: The Chicago Political Tradition*, edited by Paul M. Green and Melvin G. Holli, were crucial to understanding housing segregation in Chicago and the political career of Mayor Kennelly.

Alan M. Wald's "Willard Motley" in *Writers of the Black Chicago Renaissance*, edited by Steven C. Tracy, served as an incredibly useful survey of Motley's life and work. *Images of America: Chicago's Maxwell Street* by Lori Grove and Laura Kamedulski illuminated the feel and dynamics of the old Maxwell Street neighborhood. Motley's own survey of his life until 1940 in the *Chicago Defender*, written for his Bud Billiken fans, and his FBI file filled in the gaps regarding his life. The life of Tallulah Bankhead was largely drawn from three sources: *My Autobiography*; *Tallulah! The Life and Times of a Leading Lady*, coauthored by Joel Lobenthal; and the national edition of the *Chicago Defender* in the 1940s. Howard Greenfeld's *Ben Shahn: An Artist's Life* was a fruitful source of information on Shahn's life. *Courtroom 302* by Steve Bogira recounted the history of the Cook County Jail and the Cook County Courthouse. Arden and Gordon Lang were very gracious in discussing the family background and career of their father, Irving Lang. Mike Miller, superintendent of Division 1 of the Cook County Jail, provided Behzad Ragian and me with a tour of the old jail and gave us a detailed description of the daily life of inmates in the 1940s.

During every step of my research, I relied heavily on Chicago's daily newspapers, most importantly the *Chicago Daily Tribune*, the *Chicago Daily News*, the *Chicago Sun*, and the *Chicago Times*. I would like to thank John Culhane, a former *Chicago Daily News* reporter, for his article written in the mid-1960s, "Your Children Is Burn to Death." I am also grateful to the *Chicago Tribune* for its extensive coverage of the Valentine's Day fire in Cicero.

The holy grail of my search was the transcript of James Hickman's murder trial, for which I was, alas, unsuccessful. Under Illinois state law, unless a trial is appealed, the county clerk is not required to keep a copy of its transcript on file. Rumors and reminiscences from several people kept alive my hope that I would find the transcript, but I did not. If one ever existed in the possession of Hickman's legal team, it did not survive.

Throughout this book I have extensively quoted people whom I have never met and who, in many cases, have been deceased for decades. Each time I quote a person, I am directly sourcing a court or coroner's hearing transcript, the person's own writing, or a statement quoted in the press.

In some instances, I have used notes on interviews I made over the telephone or in person. I have made grammatical changes for the sake of clarity and brevity. I regularly consulted the *Chicago Tribune*, the *New York Times*, the *Chicago Defender*, and the *Encyclopedia Britannica* to confirm or clarify certain important historical events and dates.

I still think of this book in some ways as a work in progress, and I hope that its publication will lead to further information concerning the Hickman story. I will be happy to include any newly discovered material in a future edition.

Acknowledgments

The writing of a book is never an individual act. I could have not have completed this project without the support of many people. A few of them deserve special recognition. Behzad Ragian, my lawyer and friend, spent a considerable amount of time filing Freedom of Information Act (FOIA) requests with the City of Chicago, Cook County, and the FBI that ultimately provided the material that makes up the heart and guts of this book. Patrick M. Quinn spent many hours both copyediting the initial draft of this book and directing me to the right sources of archival material. His extensive knowledge of the older generation of American Trotskyists proved invaluable. Matt Nichter set aside the research of his own dissertation to scour the archives of the Socialist Workers Party at the Wisconsin Historical Society. Karin Baker and Jelger Kalmijn found a three-hour interview with Mike Bartell and other personal papers that filled in the gaps of his early life. Linda and Carol Myer provided me with a copy of their parents' FBI file and their father's notes on the Myer family history. The librarians of the special collections divisions of the

Daley Library at the University of Illinois at Chicago, the Chicago Historical Society, the Library of Congress, and the Harsh collection at the Chicago Public Library were extremely helpful. Mark Dickman at the Cook County Law Library generously helped me to locate legal material related to the Hickman case. Bob Quellos did a great job designing the cover of this book.

I would like to extend a special thank-you to the staff at the Cook County Medical Examiner's office for searching their warehouse and archives for the material that I needed to complete this book.

Lastly, I'd like to thank my editors at Haymarket Books, Ahmed Shawki, Paul D'Amato, Julie Fain, and Anthony Arnove. A special thanks to Ruth Goring and Dao X. Tran for extensive work on my manuscript. While many people have helped me in this project, I take responsibility for any errors.

About Haymarket Books

Haymarket Books is a nonprofit, progressive book distributor and publisher, a project of the Center for Economic Research and Social Change. We believe that activists need to take ideas, history, and politics into the many struggles for social justice today. Learning the lessons of past victories, as well as defeats, can arm a new generation of fighters for a better world. As Karl Marx said, "The philosophers have merely interpreted the world; the point, however, is to change it."

We take inspiration and courage from our namesakes, the Haymarket Martyrs, who gave their lives fighting for a better world. Their 1886 struggle for the eight-hour day, which gave us May Day, the international workers' holiday, reminds workers around the world that ordinary people can organize and struggle for their own liberation. These struggles continue today across the globe—struggles against oppression, exploitation, hunger, and poverty.

It was August Spies, one of the Martyrs targeted for being an immigrant and an anarchist, who predicted the battles being fought to this day. "If you think that by hanging us you can stamp out the labor movement," Spies told the judge, "then hang us. Here you will tread upon a spark, but here, and there, and behind you, and in front of you, and everywhere, the flames will blaze up. It is a subterranean fire. You cannot put it out. The ground is on fire upon which you stand."

We could not succeed in our publishing efforts without the generous financial support of our readers. Many people contribute to our project through the Haymarket Sustainers program, where donors receive free books in return for their monetary support. If you would like to be a part of this program, please contact us at info@haymarketbooks.org.

Shop our full catalog online at www.haymarketbooks.org or call 773-583-7884.

Also from Haymarket Books

Vietnam: The (Last) War the U.S. Lost
Joe Allen, foreword by John Pilger • In addition to debunking the popular mythology surrounding the U.S.'s longest war to date, Allen analyses three elements that played a central role in the U.S. defeat in Vietnam: the resistance of the Vietnamese, the antiwar movement in the United States, and the courageous rebellion of soldiers against U.S. military command. • ISBN 9781931859493

Breaking the Sound Barrier
Amy Goodman, edited by Denis Moynihan • Amy Goodman, award-winning host of the daily internationally broadcast radio and television program *Democracy Now!*, breaks through the corporate media's lies, sound bites, and silence in this wide-ranging new collection of articles. • ISBN 9781931859998

Essays
Wallace Shawn • In these beautiful essays acclaimed playwright and beloved actor Wallace Shawn takes readers on a revelatory journey through high art, war, politics, culture, and privilege. • ISBN 9781608460021

Hopes and Prospects
Noam Chomsky • In this urgent new book, Noam Chomsky surveys challenges such as the growing gap between North and South, American exceptionalism (including under President Barack Obama), the fiascos of Iraq and Afghanistan, the U.S.-Israeli assault on Gaza, and the recent financial bailouts. He also sees hope for the future and a way to move forward—in the democratic wave in Latin America and in the global solidarity movements that suggest "real progress toward freedom and justice." • ISBN 9781931859967

Field Notes on Democracy: Listening to Grasshoppers
Arundhati Roy • Combining fierce conviction, deft political analysis, and beautiful writing, this essential new book from Arundhati Roy examines the dark side of democracy in contemporary India. Roy looks closely at how religious majoritarianism, cultural nationalism, and neo-fascism simmer just under the surface of a country that projects itself as the world's largest democracy. • ISBN 9781608460243

Floodlines: Community and Resistance from Katrina to the Jena Six
Jordan Flaherty; foreword by Amy Goodman; preface by Tracie Washington • *Floodlines* is a firsthand account of community, culture, and resistance in New Orleans. The book weaves together the stories of gay rappers, Mardi Gras Indians, Arab and Latino immigrants, public housing residents, and grassroots activists in the years before and after Katrina. • ISBN 9781608461127

About the author

Joe Allen is the author of *Vietnam: The (Last) War the U.S. Lost* (Haymarket Books, 2008). He is a frequent contributor on criminal justice issues to the *International Socialist Review*. His article "Three Decades of Injustice: Gary Tyler Still Sits in Angola Prison" renewed national public interest in Gary's case, leading to three columns by the *New York Times'* awarding-winning columnist Bob Herbert and an exposé of the case on Amy Goodman's nationally syndicated radio program *Democracy Now!* Allen is a former member of the Teamsters and worked for several years at United Parcel Service. He has written extensively on the Teamsters at UPS, including "When Big Brown Shut Down: The UPS Strike Ten Years On." Joe Allen was born and raised in Stoughton, Massachusetts, and is the son and nephew of United States Marines. He attended the University of Massachusetts at Boston and he currently lives in Chicago.